Intimacy
BEYOND THE
BEDROOM

Intimacy
BEYOND THE
BEDROOM

ELTON PENN

Love Wins Publishing
Chandler, Arizona
www.lovewinspub.com

Printed in the United States of America

First Printing, November 2021

CONTENTS

DEDICATION   9

INTRO   13

Chapter 1   19
INTIMACY AND ITS IDENTITY

Chapter 2   25
THE BATTLE OF THE SEXES

Chapter 3   43
BEING LEFT WITHOUT,
BUT POWER WITHIN

Chapter 4   59
YOU'RE A RESULT OF
WHAT YOU'VE BEEN THROUGH

Chapter 5   75
WHAT IS YOUR TRUTH?

Chapter 6   81
THE POWER OF PRESENTATION

Chapter 7   89
ACCESS GRANTED

Chapter 8   99
FINDERS KEEPERS

Chapter 9   113
THINGS ARE NOT ALWAYS
WHAT THEY SEEM

Chapter 10   121
TO BE OR NOT TO BE

Chapter 11   133
THE (INNER) ME

Chapter 12   143
BACK TO BASICS

"Intimacy is a learned behavior that needs to be learned, relearned and displayed with every connection." Elton Penn

DEDICATION

I would like to dedicate this book to the moments in my life where I felt as though I was at my loneliest point. There were days and nights when people and family were around, and, although I was not alone, I still felt lonely. I spent my time trying to fill the many voids in my life with people and material things. I physically connected with some, mentally with others, but struggled to fully connect. Although my body was present, my mind was elsewhere — anywhere to avoid dealing with my reality.

Daily tasks, like going to work, turned into weeks and then months of going through the motions, yet I was not making any progress. It all blurred together. I was a walking shell of myself just existing, but not really living. I tried to fill my emptiness by pouring myself into others to occupy my time. I found myself constantly trying to outrun what I knew I needed to face. I needed something greater than anything physical, deeper than sex, and much more than words. I was in desperate need of something I was unable to understand or articulate.

I was attached to a number of tangible things, including being married, a manager at work, CEO of a growing non-profit organization, and a leader at church. Even though I was juggling all those titles, the circus in my head was secretly spiraling out of control. I had to admit to myself that something very significant was missing in my life.

I spent years functioning in all of my roles. I gave the appearance that I was handling everything, but things were slowly falling apart. A whole decade into marriage, it was still not what I thought it would be. I believed the day I got married would be the day all of my internal and external needs would be met, but I was mistaken. I thought untapped emotions would turn on like a light switch. On the outside, there was surface change, but on the inside, I was living a real-life Groundhog's Day. Internally, there was no change from one day to the next.

Many people would agree that church is the one place where one should be at peace. I was at church for bible study, choir rehearsal, Sunday service and different fellowship nights every single week, yet I still felt empty. My "work self" was able to show up and perform my duties. I was even promoted! Regardless of everything I was doing, I was unhappy and empty on the inside. Most nights, I found myself driving around looking for something to do or lying wide awake in bed questioning my purpose. Those sleepless nights felt like a lifetime. I would ask myself questions like, "How did it get to this point? Why do things have to be this way? When will things change?"

After years of going through, I finally got to the point where I realized some things were simply too broken to repair and I had an "aha" moment! Everything I had gone through helped me end up in a better place, spiritually, emotionally, mentally and physically. After many lonely nights, many unanswered questions, and after feeling like a failure at life, it clicked. What I needed finally stopped eluding me. What I needed was *Intimacy Beyond the Bedroom.*

INTRO

We often go through many moments in life without taking the time to understand how those moments will impact our future. Our desires of yesterday and today will directly shape what we will look for tomorrow. Whether we enjoyed or regretted our past moments, our story is our story and we cannot erase the pages from our book, as much as we would like to. While we are in a season of our life, it's hard to see how these moments will affect our decision making in the future.

Similar to my experience, most of us often fail to face the reality of a situation until we have experienced the letdown that follows it. This happens because we often look for satisfaction in people and things, neither of which have the capability of fulfilling oneself. To be honest, now I understand how some mistakes I made in the past have come from my choice to settle for external, temporary satisfaction, instead of internal fulfillment that deals with what we will later discuss, the true Inner Me.

We often struggle between making a choice from a place of desire versus a place of understanding.

Choices that come from desire lead to us choosing what feels good in the moment. When we achieve true understanding, we make choices that meet the needs of the Inner Me.

Life comes down to choices; right or wrong, good or bad, major or minor and, even, short or long-term. Many of us who have faced issues in relationships chose to rush into those relationships prematurely, instead of developing a friendship that evolved into a solid relationship. Have you ever chosen someone based on your current desire fully knowing there was no possibility of a future? Not only that, but how many times have we witnessed people, including ourselves, continuing to search for short-term jobs instead of preparing for a long-term career? We sometimes choose to spend money or time on temporary satisfaction, knowing that it won't make things better and we are still left unfulfilled.

When it comes to intimacy, it's after the hurt that we discover the need to choose carefully. Before the hurt, we choose to spend our time with people and look for what could be. Before the hurt, we tend to look past red flags and warning signs. Before the hurt, we can take people at face value. Before the hurt, we are not as skeptical when a mistake is made. It's the after effect of a negative outcome that creates a wall, making it nearly impossible to trust as you did before. Depending on the outcome, this is what causes individuals to examine what benefit the next person can offer us in the future. That's why some have become experts at identifying users early. Understanding that their whole mission is to see what they can get out of someone, but that is an entirely different book!

Have you ever wondered why men and women go through similar situations, but experience different needs? When it comes to the need for intimacy, it is often misunderstood and seen through a rose-colored lens. This lens is first obstructed by our lack of understanding about who we really are and what we really need, and then we place that obligation on others. Everyone, at one time or another, will transfer unrealistic expectations on others. These expectations can be placed deliberately, or not, and some people aren't even aware that these expectations have been placed on them.

As a man, it took me decades to understand that intimacy does not simply take place when you are physical with someone. I had many years filled with moments of physical pleasure, some of which resulted in emotional pain. I spent the better part of my twenties and thirties making decisions that, although I learned from them, I would mostly do differently today. Now, I am fully aware that intimacy does not take place simply because I have a sexual connection with someone.

How many times have you searched for and craved real intimacy? Maybe you thought you experienced intimacy, only to realize that you hadn't experienced it in its truest form. The fact of the matter is, we can spend days, weeks, and years experiencing external satisfaction with little to no intimate connection or true fulfillment. In the past, I have found myself settling for temporary satisfaction while neglecting a much deeper internal longing that went unfulfilled. Only after much self-reflection, I realized that my choices did not bring me to the place of true fulfillment that I so desperately desired.

From the moment we are born, we have natural desires and cravings. These cravings are innate like a baby crying continuously until he is fulfilled. As we get older, the desires we experience will lead us to different cravings throughout our lives. Sometimes these desires will lead us to moments of pleasure and other times they will lead us to moments of pain. After experiencing moments of pleasure, being led by my desires, and after making both good and bad choices, I noticed that each of these moments in my life ended with the same result. It is evident that, more than anything, I crave *Intimacy Beyond the Bedroom.*

CHAPTER ONE

"*Physical intimacy isn't and can never be an effective substitute for emotional intimacy.*"
John Green

INTIMACY AND ITS IDENTITY

Too often when we are trying to define intimacy, we attempt to restrict intimacy to something smaller than what it really means. We think it only means being physical with an individual. However, true intimacy includes what one experiences internally, and externally, through the power of connection. This is not limited to an experience with another person, but most importantly, it has to do with what one eventually realizes within.

Intimacy is defined as familiarity, closeness, understanding, relationship, and confidence. It can be viewed as having a connection with oneself or with someone else. Intimacy is to know and be known, without the fear of rejection. Unfortunately, many of us find out too late that we cannot share intimacy with another, until we first discover the value of knowing ourselves.

How ironic is it that we expect and yearn for fulfillment from someone else, but we have yet to discover and experience self-fulfillment? Although I had some idea of the true meaning of intimacy, it wasn't until my late 30s that I questioned how often I chose to sacrifice intimacy for temporary pleasure. I believed that with age and experience, a person would have learned how to be intimate in a relationship with someone. But, how do you know something if it was never shared or taught? How can a man be intimate with his wife when he'd never seen intimacy displayed? How can a woman utilize another method of intimacy, other than sex, when the only thing she'd witnessed was women using sex as a means to feel love or self-worth? When a person comes to a point where they know, and feel, that things are not right within, it becomes evident that something has to change. The hard part is taking that first step towards the change one wants to see.

Many times, we leave intimacy in the control of someone else and we relinquish our power of being enough. A person should never give someone else the power to determine what you deem your self-worth to be, what makes you feel valued, and what makes you who you are — especially when you have discovered it yourself. When you crave intimacy, you learn that sharing a moment with someone does not necessarily make the moment intimate. You learn that you can be physically attracted to someone, but still be internally turned off at the same time. Therefore, what makes the moment intimate is not what's on the outside, but the connection you experience with someone on the inside.

I spent many days and nights wanting, desiring, and, even craving, intimacy. I wondered if I was worthy of receiving intimacy, if I had ever experienced it, why others appeared to experience it, and how long it would take for me to experience the intimacy that I so desperately needed.

I remember there were times when my ex-wife and I were in the same space, but our minds were worlds apart. There were moments when she or I wanted to be vulnerable for the sake of obtaining some type of affection, but neither of us said or did anything to receive the affection we desired. Although we were parents who had past relationship experience, we lacked the tools needed (communication, trust, and love) to do the required work in the relationship. Consequently, we failed to express our desires to each other.

We were reluctant to expose ourselves to one another because we did not want to risk being rejected. There were moments where we wanted to be held by each other, but didn't feel secure enough in our relationship to ask for it. Security in relationships is what opens the door to healthy communication, where both people can be honest and vulnerable with each other.

CHAPTER

TWO

"Nobody will ever win the battle of the sexes. There is too much fraternizing with the enemy."
Henry Kissinger

THE BATTLE OF THE SEXES

Have you ever wanted the ability to read the minds of the opposite sex in order to better understand what they were thinking? There is a great book written by John Gray titled, "Men Are from Mars and Women Are from Venus." The overall theme of the book is to help men and women understand the perspectives of the opposite sex and to show them how there is a vast difference in the way men and women view and handle things.

As a man, I can honestly say that men have a hard time understanding intimacy apart from the physical aspect and some women feel the same. Let me be clear: although a man may engage sexually with a woman, that does not automatically equate to intimacy. There are times when both men and women settle for something sexual and not share an intimate connection with the other person.

Have you ever noticed that even when one is honest about their intentions being merely physical, sometimes the other person may try to suppress their feelings? That only lasts so long before ending in disappointment. For the most part, women are known for wanting more of a commitment before allowing sex to enter the relationship. Barbara Cartland says, "Among men, sex sometimes results in intimacy; among women, intimacy sometimes results in sex." Honestly speaking, men are not initially intimate, which is the culprit behind women making the mistake of placing all men in the same shallow category. However, the truth is that most men, including myself, were not taught how to be intimate, only physical. Furthermore, I can say for myself that I did not see examples of what intimacy truly is.

A key element to true intimacy is a true knowledge of self. I also never knew that intimacy extended past the physical aspect of a relationship. If we were to ask a group of men and women how often they had been intimate with their partners, you would quickly find that men specifically have a limited understanding of what intimacy really is. When I was a young man, my father never taught me the values of knowing myself or women. Later in life, I realized how my parents could have played an important role in teaching me, through demonstration, the characteristics of intimacy. Instead, I found myself as an adult unequipped while simultaneously attempting to develop or maintain relationships in my ignorance.

Years later, I was counseling people based on what I learned in school, what I personally experienced, in addition to what I had come to know through the experiences of others. I recall speaking with a woman, who we will call Debbie, who finally admitted, only after nearly a year of counseling, that she was molested and raped by her father. Debbie had been married for over five years and still struggled to share an intimate moment with her husband. Debbie's husband wanted to have kids. However, she found it difficult to separate being raped by her father from making love with her husband. She loved her husband, but could not make herself share her past with her husband because she saw how her husband loved and respected her dad. This left her husband losing a fight before he even stepped into the ring. Her inability to articulate her feelings made him question her faithfulness and even her love for him. He never truly understood the reason for her insecurity and the lack of desire she had for intimacy. Because he was confused by her inability to be intimate with him, Debbie's husband questioned if they were meant to be together or not. Her actions did not start with him, but lingered from her past which was filled with unaddressed issues.

There was another young lady who we will call Sarah. She was 25 and had little to no knowledge of intimacy. Sarah, like Debbie, viewed intimacy through the lens of her past, which was filled with unaddressed issues. She was seeing a young man who she had known for only two weeks. After having sex, he immediately left her. Because he left so quickly, she was left feeling inadequate and empty. Without knowing why he left, she was left to reconcile her feelings of abandonment, which she experienced in her childhood, as well as her feelings of rejection. Sarah's father was not in her life as a child. There were uncles and other men who were a part of her life, but it never filled the void of her absent father. She was confused and did not understand the ongoing problem of men disappearing and not playing an active part in her life. In her mind, she thought that she received what she needed in those meaningless experiences. As a 25-year-old with multiple short-lived relationships, she became okay with the temporary satisfaction of sex and began to settle for physical relationships to gain a true understanding of intimacy. Although everything in our past may not be resolved, we must make an effort to be honest with ourselves about it. When we recognize the issues from our past and how they impact our relationships, only then can we address them.

I remember having a conversation with a friend about our history with our fathers. We both realized that we wished our parents would have shown more love to us and our families. Now, as adults, we were wrestling with how our dads expected us to understand their different displays of love towards us. We knew our dads loved us, although their actions showed different. My dad would disappear for days and weeks at a time, then appear with gifts or treats. His dad, on the contrary, was physically abusive, but would label the abuse as "tough love."

It was not until much later in my adulthood that I understood that our fathers did love us; they just did not know that we needed to see and feel that love through their interactions as well. Not having that love as a child made it more difficult for us to show, and accept, love from others. As we sat there and continued reminiscing, we became emotionally overwhelmed and the tears started flowing. We thought about how desperately we desired and longed for their love, even until that very day. It was also apparent that we, as parents ourselves, wanted to show and give love to our own children, but still did not know how. Even though we were both married with kids, it became clearer that we were still affected by the absence of those feelings from our parents. I also realized something even greater in that moment. I realized that one can be single or in a relationship and still lack intimacy.

Just because someone is in a relationship doesn't mean they honestly know how to show love or be loved. As my friend and I discussed our desire for love and intimacy, we continued to look back at our childhood. Neither of us could remember our parents ever hugging us, showing us affection, or telling us how much they loved us. We couldn't even recall moments where our parents simply said, "I'm proud of you," or "I love you." However, what we vividly remembered was their inability to express their emotions to us. This caused both of us to develop issues with acknowledging our feelings and expressing them to the people we love. As much as we truly wanted to be different from our parents and walk a different path and as much as we tried to not make the same mistakes they did, we both had to admit that we had similarities.

I remember when my first daughter was born, I thought I would be unlike my dad. I vowed to never leave my daughter and to always be supportive. My mistake, like many men, was thinking that my presence alone was evidence of my love for her. Unbeknownst to me, I still did not know how to affirm her and show her my love. As I look back, I realize that I had many misconceptions and made numerous mistakes because of my childhood.

One common mistake made by adults is centered

around the mindset that being present is enough. In my life, I found that parents, companions, and friends can be present and of great benefit, but still may not have the power to help you become your best self. I have learned that moments make memories. How could this information shape the idea of intimacy in my daughter's life? I was someone who should have made her comfortable with being hugged. I should have taught her that even when vulnerability is perceived negatively, at times, it can also be positive. Unfortunately, I failed to demonstrate that to her.

I vividly remember being able to discipline her for doing wrong, but I still struggled to display my love for her and my pride when she would accomplish things or do something right. I demonstrated those same mannerisms when dealing with my other daughters, my ex-wife and in prior relationships. Thirteen years later, I was blessed with another daughter and I approached parenting situations much differently; armed with the knowledge of what I failed to do the first time around. I had so many opportunities to teach her what real intimacy is and the value of self-worth. Demonstrating how to share a closeness with someone that goes deeper than the superficial. It took me decades to realize that many of my characteristics mirrored those of my parents. Even though I hadn't lived with either of my parents since I was seven years old, my mother's admiration for family and my dad's work ethic poured out of me. Unfortunately, my mother's ability to emotionally disconnect and my dad's commitment issues shone through just as bright.

Characteristic traits from our parents are real! Regardless of physical presence, traits have the ability to show up and show through offspring. One of my daughters has not had a relationship with her father for some time, yet, according to my wife, she walks like, laughs like, and has many of the same thought processes as her biological father. The absence of being shown intimacy in my childhood made it nearly impossible for me to teach it, or show it, to my kids. After I remarried, I had an epiphany; my inability to be intimate with others was really based on my lack of understanding of what true intimacy is and not that I did not want to be intimate.

Intimacy can be uncomfortable, depending on your past. Intimacy can be anything from holding hands, to cuddling, to simply being able to look a person in the eye to express your feelings. My epiphany came after my personal counseling sessions, coupled with the numerous counseling sessions I conducted with women, men and couples. The same "issues" kept rising; she wanted him to show more affection and to feel loved, he wanted to feel respected and for her to be more understanding that what he was giving was all he believed he had to give. It became quite clear to me that women had a better understanding of true intimacy than men and men's comprehension of real intimacy wasn't even close to what women understood!

The majority of these battles during counseling revolved around the individuals' mindset and past patterns. Understanding that intimacy is not gender specific was one of life's toughest lessons for me. Both men and women alike find it hard to display or receive affection at times, but men more so than women. I experienced a lot of physical connections with various women.

I found it easy to share sexual encounters without intimacy. I spent nights with women who wanted more than I could give. There were women who truly believed I was the right man for them, without knowing deep down I had major insecurities about my ability to have and maintain any type of relationship. Letting go became second nature, in order to disguise my insecurities, leaving women wondering why things didn't work out.

Have you ever noticed how easy it is for some individuals to move on to a new relationship or move on after things don't work out and you're left stuck, second guessing yourself? Sadly, the investment for one is not the same for another. It's still a phenomenon; trying to understand how you can spend time getting to know someone only to find out that you didn't really know them at all. Although the relationship is what they wanted, I knew inside the true limitation of what I could give. I found it easy to move from one encounter to the next because company is what I settled for, but they desired a committed relationship.

If knowing is half the battle, then what we don't know is what causes us to ask so many questions about something we don't understand. The battle of the sexes has to do with an inner power struggle; a struggle that can only be fought when we understand the different opponents involved in the battle. On the one hand, there's a battle within ourselves and then there's a battle to fulfill the need and understanding of the other person involved. The ability to give or get intimacy from a companion without allowing them to know your truth will lead to a lack of fulfillment. In essence, trying to get something you need from someone else when you don't even know what you need is impossible. Without understanding, there can be no growth. How can there be achievement when there's no known goal to reach? There can't be! Your truth regarding your past pain, struggles, and insecurities that were never addressed and unresolved are the very reason why the same issues resurface in the present. These issues can even become generational.

Some of us have suppressed past molestation, rape, abandonment, physical and verbal abuse, domestic violence, and a number of other things. The fact remains that we often try to appear as if things are great on the outside because we want to appear more whole than we really are. Some of us have experienced the struggle of a single-parent household, having both parents in the home, but never present in your life, or not growing up with our parents at all. It's not until later in life when we start to notice how struggle arises from issues we saw growing up with our parents —single, married, happy, unhappy, faithful and unfaithful. Whatever your experience, it's important to know that it can manifest itself in your relationships. Not only that, but we fail to realize how much our past experiences influence our actions today. They cause us to battle inwardly with how we handle present situations. Too many times we fail to

Side note:
Not receiving affirmation as a child can leave scars we are unaware of. Those scars leave us as adults needing affirmation from people and things without understanding why.

understand that the battle is not always with the opposite sex, or the struggle in finding a mate. Before finding a companion, we have to learn the importance of keeping yourself company in the interim and appreciate the value within you. We also need to understand that, a battle develops with the opposite sex when we are unwilling to expose ourselves to them, allowing them to see what we truly battle with on a personal level. Exposure causes feelings of vulnerability. For example, if a woman expresses to her man that, when she was a little girl, she felt safest when her dad was at home when she went to sleep for the night. She is equating protection for her to a man being present when she turns in for the night. If, after expressing that to her man, he continues to stay out all night, every night, and she goes to sleep without him, the woman no longer feels protected by him and the battle is no longer theirs, but his to own.

Side note:
Being truthful about who you are is a vulnerability that should be dealt with prior to settling down with someone, to avoid the obstacles that come with hiding your true self. Your truth is worth taking the time to understand.

It's not just about knowing the what, but the why, and how it must be addressed as well, or it could be seen as a battle for control. Although we may never fully understand the what, the why, and the how of a particular issue, we must understand that in order for us to be better for someone else, we must first do the work to become better for ourselves. Change needs to start with a desire to better ourselves for our own happiness, which could then benefit another person. Too many times when we fail to see change, we think it's not worth it to continue trying. The truth could be the simple fact that change is not easy when we're used to being who we've been and doing what we've done for years.

Consider also that they may see nothing wrong with themselves and are not motivated to change. Changing a mindset, a pattern, a behavior, or a practice is not a quick fix, nor can it be accomplished overnight. We often run into problems when we superficially change verses the effort that has to be made to internally change for yourself rather than for the sake of someone else. The battle we face relating to the lack of intimacy may cause us to look at the opposite sex as the opponent when that's not the case; they're simply different. As opposite as two individuals may be, that does not mean they're in opposition to each other. Opposite is defined as a person or thing that is totally different from, or the reverse of, someone or something else. Opponent is defined as someone who competes against or fights another in a contest, game, or argument; a rival or adversary.

Side note: When you believe you are in a relationship, and it's a continual battle against an opponent, you have to know when to change direction.

It's ok for a couple to be opposites, but they should not be opponents. Perspectives need to change before the battle can be won with the desired results. For example, my current wife's love language is physical touch. In the beginning of our relationship, I was not as affectionate as she wanted me to be. Once I made the decision to love her the way she needed to be loved, I was able to hold her hand without her asking, kiss her when she least expected it, and know when she needed me to pull her close. Without the change in my mind, there would have been no change in my affection towards her. I learned the battle was not with her or my past relationships, it became a battle the moment I decided to allow myself to live and love her, despite my past. As long as I was not trying to be better there was no battle to fight. The moment I decided to take action to change is when the battle began. If the only love we show is the only love we've experienced, we run the risk of shortchanging our partner, and ourselves, of endless possibilities.

Intimacy is a learned behavior that needs to be learned, relearned and displayed with every connection. It's not something we automatically know how to display or share, not to mention understanding the other person's perception of intimacy. While growing up, I cannot recall a single time where I saw my dad, granddad, or uncles display affection and intimacy to their spouse. In fact, my very first sexual experience, at the age of 16 with an older woman, was far from intimate. She taught me how to sexually please a woman, but that was all.

Side note:
When we fail to communicate honestly, problems don't magically go away. They turn into walls that keep everything locked in and the other person left out.

I saw inadequacies when I tried to display intimacy when it came to everyone I loved, not just women.my I had no desire for it, nor did I know how to have an intimate connection with a woman that didn't include being sexual. When we are not honest with ourselves, we live a lie about who we truly are.

As embarrassing as it is, I remember times in our marriage when my ex-wife longed for my touch. She wanted things from me that were normal for any couple, like sitting close while watching a movie or simply wanting to be held, but I struggled because of my own issues. I made excuses or would walk with my hands in my pocket to avoid having to hold hands or to deal with the real struggle within myself.

Countless times I would ask myself why I couldn't communicate honestly to her about how uncomfortable it made me feel to simply hold hands. Why did I let my past affect my ability to experience in my adult years? My refusal to acknowledge my truth hurt her and destroyed our relationship. Here's a word of caution: be careful to not allow your reasons to become your excuses. Above all, do not allow the small things that annoy you to become the proverbial straw that breaks the camel's back in your relationship.

Every little thing my ex-wife did wrong was a major problem in my sight. For years I found myself holding on to even the smallest of things, with an inability to let them go. I found myself staying mad for weeks at a time at the smallest issue, all because I was internally not happy.

Sidenote: Teaching someone how to physically please you does not necessarily increase their understanding of intimacy.

Now, it is easy for you to see how I didn't handle my situation well. What things have happened to you in your past that cause problems for you now, that you cannot see or admit? This is the question that I hope you'll be willing to answer honestly before you end this book. That answer and many others will help you to avoid cycles that affect so many individuals over and over again. Change is one of the themes throughout this book and it is a common situation that affects so many lives every day. It is easy for us to see reasons why other people need to change, or reasons why they are wrong, but we cannot do this without addressing the issues we have ourselves.

Let's go back to my issue with avoidance. Looking deeper, I realize that it wasn't as simple as not wanting to be touched by my ex-wife. It stemmed from not knowing the true intimacy that comes through connecting with her in any other way besides sex. If the only connection you have with a person is sexual or superficial small talk, or anything else that does not come with embracing each other's truth, I would say you need to learn how to be intimate. Unfortunately, there are many people that have felt, or are currently experiencing, the same emotions I had with no change in sight. The only difference is, they do a much better job of hiding or suppressing their issues. Regrettably, my facial expressions and body language would constantly tell how I really felt.

The battle of the sexes really forces us to understand how different women and men perspectives are when it comes to our way of thinking, including the ways we need and display intimacy. As a man, I remember longing for respect in my relationships with women. Inversely, they longed for affection; quiet moments of intimacy, and conversation. Even though I also wanted affection, intimacy and conversation, I did not know how to communicate that I lacked understanding of how to be intimate without being sexual. Time and time again, we clashed because I was fruitless in understanding the importance of owning my truth.

As a result of not loving myself, I struggled to love others. Understanding intimacy, and how your partner needs you to display it to them, is more important than you know. The why is something that can be discussed later, but should not be the reason we fail to provide it. Additionally, the why behind your partner needing intimacy from you, is a vital component to maintaining healthy relationships. We should take the time to understand how significant intimacy is to ourselves first, then our relationship. After we understand intimacy and we grasp the value of it individually, then we would realize that effective, honest communication is vital to the health of any relationship. The main point of intimacy is to establish a connection that goes beyond the bedroom. The problem is that some of us fail to see how past, unresolved issues can negatively contribute to broken relationships and future disappointment.

Side note
Being truthful about who you are is a vulnerability that should be dealt with prior to settling down with someone, to avoid the obstacles that come with hiding your true self. Your truth is worth taking the time to understand.

This is where most of our problems lie — the battle of the sexes. As painful as it may be, we need to acknowledge and address our individual issues or we can never be successful in having a healthy, fulfilling relationship with someone.

CHAPTER THREE

"I used to think the worst thing in life was to end up all alone; it's not. The worst thing in life is to end up with people that make you feel all alone."
Robin Williams

BEING LEFT WITHOUT, BUT POWER WITHIN

Have you ever been left alone, but still didn't feel lonely? Intentionally or unintentionally not dating, and you are left alone, forced into a new reality? At times we search for relationships and companionship because we believe it will be the determining factor that allows us to obtain fulfillment. There's a level of peace and a place in life where we decide not to settle, regardless of how it appears to others. Explaining your actions to others who might think that something is wrong with you is difficult. Explaining to them is irrelevant when you know your value. On this level, however, you know that this is the best decision for you, but you're alone. You're independent, but alone. You're goal driven, but alone. Hardworking, yet alone. Intelligent and strong, but still alone. This is where some, if not most, of my mistakes have happened. Many times, I would make decisions regarding companionship only to find out that even while spending time with someone, there was still something vital and significant missing. We give people the benefit of the doubt, even when we have a gut feeling--- an alarm that we often ignore due to our curiosity. We disregard the internal warning signs but are still curious; advised against it, but we can't walk away.

I married my ex-wife at the age of 26. This was after counseling, prayer, and after we decided that we were ready for all that marriage would bring. Reality hit me on the first night of our honeymoon that I had made a lifelong commitment for which I was not prepared. Nor did I truly recognize the vast differences in our maturity levels.

The first night of our honeymoon, I found myself out roaming the streets of Hawaii. She was tired after a long weekend and wanted to rest. I, on the other hand, wanted to keep the party going. Even when we returned home from the honeymoon, I continued as a night owl. I made superficial adjustments but failed to mentally and emotionally adjust to having a spouse. There was no change in my mindset and no change in my behavior. I was still out roaming the streets at night, looking for anything to do to avoid the reality that I was not ready for the commitment that marriage required. I filled my days and nights with any and everything I could, in order to avoid dealing with my resistance to the maturity that needed to take place. The truth was, although I was married, I still lacked the maturity needed to build and maintain a healthy marriage. Yes, we would sporadically do things as a

> "Some steps need to be taken alone. It's the only way to really figure out where you need to go and who you need to be." – Mandy Hale

family — dinner, movies or game night — that appeared fulfilling, but to me, it was an ongoing struggle to maintain being married. Those struggles had to do with me wanting to party and wanting to stay at home with my family. I chose to be with friends instead of enjoying the time with my family.

Take, for instance, the butterfly. Butterflies don't begin their lives as colorful, flying insects. Their transformation manifests via four different stages during their lifetime; egg, larva, pupa, and then full-grown butterfly. Unfortunately, some people haven't grown out of their adolescent stage, despite their age; a full-grown adult with a childlike mindset.

As I reflect on growth and mindset, I remember how I spent years working, dining, and sharing moments with my ex-wife, only to find that we were never comfortable enough to be willfully vulnerable with each other. After years of being married and going to counseling, I remember my ex-wife and I having many conversations, attempting to fix our problems.

Side note: If you're not willing to grow and mature in your mindset, you can't expect great outcomes because they only come as result of the effort you put in.

We made several attempts to get on the same page, only to find ourselves in what seemed like two separate books all together. Talking, but not listening; together, yet so far apart. Some conversations were good, but we walked away from other conversations without an agreement or understanding. In essence, one of us really didn't want to do it, but to avoid further argument, we would simply move on, never really resolving anything.

We both deeply desired better, but we had no tools to work through those crucial conversations to make things better. Like many others, this led to us pointing fingers at one another, talking at each other rather than listening with the intent to truly understand the other perspective. It's interesting to look back and realize that after all those conversations neither of us understood what our partner needed and wanted. This was not because we did not care about each other, but when you do not understand or are afraid to be vulnerable with each other, you often find yourself left without true change. We found ourselves holding onto many unspoken needs, thoughts, feelings, pains, and frustrations. At the time, those emotions felt like, and appeared to have been, too difficult to communicate. However, this left the other person with no way to fix, help, or change the situation. We were left without because neither of us knew how to articulate how our individual need for *Intimacy Beyond the Bedroom* was not being fulfilled by the other. We lived in the same home, slept in the same bed, but couldn't penetrate the emotional and mental barriers built up over time. We would get mad at each other and go days without talking or touching. We spent days and weeks going about our lives pretending that everything was alright to those outside looking in. With all the internal issues going on in our marriage, we couldn't see that the lack of intimacy was a sign of other issues coming from a deeper place within both of us.

There were foolish mistakes that I made that I can now attribute to my immaturity. There were many nights that my ex-wife assumed I was at a club or with someone else. In reality, there were so many nights I spent driving around looking for anything to do, silently crying out, wishing things were different, tired of the ongoing feelings of failure and loneliness.

"We can see more through our tears than we can through a telescope"
-Bruce Lee

When you are blinded by feelings, your ability to see things clearly will be hindered. I learned so much about myself the more time I spent alone. The pain of being left without forced me to focus inwardly on several things I misunderstood about myself. For instance, I remember thinking that just because I was an adult, the affirmation I didn't receive as a kid was something that I no longer needed. Once I realized I was not receiving it in my marriage, I started seeking affirmation from the outside. Although I was without the affirmation in my marriage, I had the power within to communicate it to her, but I refused to be vulnerable.

I also thought I needed to hide my feelings. I was shown that real men did not show emotions and, if they did, they were weak. When the truth of the matter is, what makes us human is our ability to feel and express our emotions. Intimacy requires an

Sidenote:
You have to be willing to release in order to gain. Holding on, holds up the process of becoming better.

understanding of oneself. You need the time to truly know yourself before trying to give what you do not understand to someone else.

To appreciate *Intimacy Beyond the Bedroom*, you must be willing to be honest about the past as well as your understanding, or lack of, of what you desire. You have to be cognizant of the absence, or presence, of past intimacy and know how that will translate into your current relationship.

You really need to acknowledge the issues of past hurt and disappointment; it's what makes us who we are. Unfortunately, the unmet desire for intimacy can be experienced in singleness or in a relationship with little to no fulfillment. How awful it is to have physical experiences with others, but still feel no companionship?

Side note: What you desire today, has much to do with what you experienced yesterday.

Over the course of writing this book, I took a random survey of women and men ranging from teens to seniors. What I found is that, most of us don't want to admit that we spend a good amount of our time with people who leave us without power, peace, happiness, and fulfillment. We lack the understanding, and the knowledge, that we have the power within ourselves to change how we feel. Because we are unwilling to face the reality of a situation, we will be left with unmet needs, settling for years. Oftentimes, after compromising values, beliefs, and standards for the desire for intimacy, we end up losing pieces of ourselves. The problem is that we often end up alone, or in relationships, with pieces still missing. Put your situation into perspective; it does not make sense to live with missing pieces and live alone. If you're going to be alone anyway, why not do the work in putting the pieces into their respective places? If we're honest, you know when something is missing, even if you cannot put your finger on what that something is at that moment.

This rule of thumb is not just for relationships, but applies to those who fail to speak up for themselves, those who are passive, those who allow others to run over them, those who act nonchalantly about everything, those who are too quick to become angry and those who wallow in their insecurities. You can insert whatever your truth is, but it is only when you're able to acknowledge that "when this happens, I feel this," whether good or bad, that you can begin to utilize the power within.

Side note:
While you have the time, invest in yourself. Who better to invest in you, than you? No one!

There are times when we, as individuals, need to stop trying to fix only what the eye can see, and admit that it's time for us to work on bettering ourselves, starting from the inside out. This speaks to what I refer to as the Inner Me (which we will discuss later in the book). Self-deception largely contributed to who I was and who I portrayed myself to be. Like in my previous marriage, many of us avoid addressing issues in relationships on all levels. At times, we avoid confrontation simply because our minds are made up that it has to work. When we're not honest, we end up trying to address superficial things in order to compensate for the lack of fulfillment regarding real issues. For me, I remember arguing over so many unimportant things, all the while avoiding issues that were vital to the wellbeing of our relationship.

In essence, I was delaying the necessary work that I needed to do which would have led me to the root of my own issues. I had years of stuff that I held on to, from my childhood to my adult life. Despite efforts to free myself from the prison of the past, I found myself emotionally crippled. I was blocked by unforgiveness, bitterness, resentment, hurt, and anger. My previous marriage surprisingly lasted for ten years. After the divorce, I would periodically find myself replaying past conversations, arguments, and other scenarios wondering how the relationship went so wrong. Many of those situations could have been handled better, but I lacked the maturity, and the knowledge, to address things differently.

I found myself wondering how a relationship that, at one time, appeared to be so right, ended up feeling so wrong? I was searching for answers while still trying to comprehend that just because two people appear to be facing the same way does not mean that they're headed in the same direction. I now know that neither of us was wrong or right. We were just two different people on two different levels with different experiences from our past that impacted each other differently. As different as we were, we should have been trying to embrace the value of being different; having thoughts and ideas that complemented one another.

It has been said that opposites attract, but in a relationship, those opposites should bring balance, creating an atmosphere of unity. Oftentimes, being opposite in your core beliefs creates an unhealthy imbalance. Unfortunately, in my case, we were unable to compromise for the sake of saving the relationship. We spent so much time trying to make one puzzle out of two different puzzles without properly connecting the pieces to form a new, better puzzle.

Now, I can look back and admit that even after the divorce, I had years of resentment underneath the surface that had nothing to do with my ex-wife. That resentment was a piece of the puzzle that should have been acknowledged and dealt with prior to marriage. Even after being married for some years, we knew the relationship was over but we faltered along halfheartedly. I can't speak for her, but I can remember constantly asking myself if I should leave or should I stay. It's so interesting that most of us will stay connected to individuals to avoid dealing with ourselves and the truth behind our reality. The reality is that it's highly possible that you can have a healthy relationship with someone else. The reality may be that you've spent years, that you can't get back, and now you have to start over. When we're left with no choice but to spend time alone, we're forced to explore the parts of

Sidenote:
Knowing when to leave is important!

us that make decisions, ignore the obvious, and deny the truth, even if it's uncomfortable.

Intimacy Beyond the Bedroom is not about sex! Let me say that again: *Intimacy Beyond the Bedroom* is not about sex! It is not about the physical side of a relationship and it is not even about another person. It's about acknowledging that there is a part of us that has cravings and that demands our attention.

The truth is that most of us are searching for intimacy, but can only see it coming from others, especially when we don't understand intimacy ourselves. People are quick to offer relationship advice that they don't take themselves and we are quick to see what the other person could do better, while individually in need of major repair. We think we want intimacy, yet we are ill prepared to do the work it takes to experience it.

We jump at the opportunity of getting to know someone, yet we still don't understand ourselves. How hasty we are to want someone with no baggage, no hurt, and no trauma yet we ourselves come with a laundry list of damaged goods. *Intimacy Beyond the Bedroom* should be the path we take with ourselves before we initiate it with someone else. Sex was not a problem within my marriage, until we allowed ourselves to sleep with issues in between us. The intimacy needed in our relationship extended past the bedroom. We missed opportunities to build the other person's dreams in addition to helping the other person to accomplish their personal goals. When intimacy is understood and you are free in a relationship, opinions are wanted and not discouraged. Individuals don't lose their identities, but are embraced for who you are and what you bring to the table. Intimacy requires trust and complete buy-in from both people.

We need to clear up the notion that two, half persons make up a whole relationship. Teddy Pendergrass had it all wrong when he sang about "50/50 love." Think about it; do you really want 50% from your partner? Of course not! The truth is that both people should be whole before pursuing a relationship. One mistake we made prior to marriage was attempting to build a strong marriage with no tools to maintain it. I now understand that you can marry a good person and you can have good intentions, but without the right tools, you will not get good results. Most of the tools I thought I had, were taken from what I observed from other people, but those tools were never in my possession. Other tools involved words that I heard had worked for other people, yet they were still not in my possession. After trying to use the tools that I observed from others, after attempting to do the things that I learned, and after making an effort to experience more intimate moments, I still was left without knowing how to use the tools. It was like having a wound that needed attention. I had the tools (stitches, sutures, bandage, tourniquet, etc.), but I didn't know how to properly diagnose my wound to apply the necessary level of care. Can you imagine needing a tourniquet, yet you've applied a bandage while you're actually bleeding out? Yes, the thought is ridiculous; the wrong treatment could result in irreparable damage. The continual misdiagnosis prevented me from releasing the power of intimacy within.

There was a point where I didn't have family around. My brothers had their own families to take care of, my ex-wife and daughters lived in another city, and I was left living alone and dealing with those issues that resided deep inside of me. There were things that I'm ashamed of and things that I wish I could simply forget.

For years I attempted to cover up the hurt and pain in my life by masking it with having people around me. After the crowd died down, after acquiring a DUI, after having to sit in a jail cell overnight, I was all alone. There was nothing left except my thoughts; I felt completely empty. I felt powerless to make myself whole, but realized how much I needed this time to search for those missing puzzle pieces.

Being left alone and without was a blessing in disguise. When I was finally alone, I had no choice but to start over, rebuild, and reflect on things that happened throughout my life leading up to this point. I was without all the people and things that I thought would be in my life forever. I understand that there are reasons and seasons for both people and things. As much as it hurts, I can honestly say that the hurt caused me to recognize the true power that was inside me.

Most of us would not have achieved, would not have excelled, would not have changed, and would not have made the needed adjustments in our lives if people, circumstances, and things remained the same. Whatever your "thing" is (mine was divorce, yours could be losing your job, someone else's could be the loss of a family member), when it happens, and it literally shatters all your hope and ability to see the bright side of things, that's when the power that lies within has to be released — even if it is painful.

The saying "no pain, no gain" continues to be true. When we are forced to make a hard decision or find an answer, that's when most of us find out what we are really made of. My encouragement for you, after attempting to disguise my insecurity and feelings of inadequacy is, don't allow your pride or fear to get in the way of change. Making the right change can potentially propel you towards greatness. Although you are left without, the power found within gives you the space to reflect. Use the power within to make the change. Take the necessary time and effort needed to fix yourself. All too often, we want people to take us to a place we have yet to experience ourselves and show us things we failed to see on our own. All because we've settled, for so long, for superficial forms of intimacy rather than pursuing a true knowledge of what *Intimacy Beyond the Bedroom* really is.

Most people don't believe they have the power to change things for the better, but they do. Your pathway to change may not look like everyone else's, but you have power within you to move to a place of fulfillment in yourself and in your relationships.

CHAPTER

FOUR

"Some of the best lessons we ever learn are learned from past mistakes. The error of the past is the wisdom and success of the future."
Dale Turner

YOU ARE THE RESULT OF WHAT YOU'VE BEEN THROUGH

How many times have you said, "That won't be my story," when discussing what you experienced as a child, in a relationship or just in life? It's interesting how our past experiences have a way of shaping our thinking and behavior today. As time passes, our choices and decisions change as a result of what we experience over time. Based on those experiences, we either do one of three things; grow through it to become a better person, allow those experiences to change us for the worse, or we simply don't evolve at all.

Because we naturally gravitate towards familiarity, we often end up dealing with the same experiences we witnessed in the past. We follow the steps of the examples displayed to us or we make attempts to live our lives differently. If we truly learn from our history, we can avoid repeating the same mistakes. The key is to learn from those mistakes so history does not repeat itself. If you pay close attention, most actions and decisions are observed behaviors, learned over a period of time, or things demonstrated to us and subconsciously in our mind by our unique experiences. Our experiences are not always a matter of choice, as we are not given the opportunity to choose our upbringing.

Based on your experience, if you had the choice, would you have chosen a different upbringing? Not necessarily your family members, but your experiences and circumstances? If we had to describe the process of learning about intimacy and how we learned to be intimate from our influencers, we would realize that some of us never witnessed it in our homes, but from going through various experiences over time. Most of us choose to connect with individuals based on our past experiences and our influencers, without even knowing. How we currently handle things often stems from our past. This is especially true when it comes to people and things that we like and dislike. Although we try not to, we usually end up making choices similar to what happened in our past, such as settling for someone we don't really want to be with or choosing someone who is not a good fit for us.

For instance, people who said they would never have a mate who abuses them, yet they end up marrying an abuser or people who said they never wanted to marry someone who had an addiction, but end up marrying an addict. Growing up, I saw how my grandmother treated my grandfather and I always said I would never stay in a marriage where the two of us were unhappy. I failed to live up to that statement and my first marriage ended. After much reflection, I realized that most of the pain, lies, and deceit were caused by me. Sadly, I had become the person I never imagined I would be— a man with faulty character.

When I initially started to write this book, I found myself struggling to share my experiences. I wondered if the things I've gone through would benefit others. If you don't take anything else from this book, you need to know, what you have gone through is of great benefit to someone else. Your journey is valuable. Two of the biggest issues I had were my immaturity and lack of honesty, which contributed to the marriage not working. For years I hesitated to share my experiences with others because of the fear that I would never recover from their opinions (we will talk about this later in the book, but I think it's worth mentioning here.)

Side note: If you have yet to follow your own advice, stop giving it!

When we care more about living a lie than about being honest with ourselves, that is an area that needs attention. We need to be ever cognizant of how our past significantly impacts our present.

Some of the hardest moments in my life had a way of bringing the best out of me, even though that was not what I saw or believed at the time. What we go through not only has the opportunity to benefit us personally, but it can also be of great benefit to others. What seems like a hard situation today may be a difficult and lonely point in your life, but I've learned that the darkest point is right before dawn.

For years I listened to people who would offer advice in areas they had yet to conquer for themselves. People often advise you without having complete knowledge, and while their advice regarding your situation sounds good to them, it doesn't mean things will work out for your good.

People are quick to instruct others based on how they see it and how they feel. However, I've learned that we should be careful how we receive advice and advise others. Consideration has to be based on the individual's success and failures on the matter. It's important to remember that even sound advice is filled with regret, fear, and frustration. It's also filled with thoughts of "I wish I would have" or "I should have." Before you give advice, you need to consider how valid it is. Are you "living proof," or are you still in the midst of your storm?

Sound advice should be based on truth, current or past experience, and knowledge. For example, you cannot soundly advise someone how to get out of an abusive relationship when you're still currently in an abusive relationship. You could, however, advise them on warning signs and behaviors of such a relationship.

When we honestly examine our decisions, we find them filled with so many different types of emotions we wrestle with trying to figure out all the perplexing details of our quandary. Many of our experiences have left scars that go beyond the physical. In fact, those scars leave us internally wounded, mentally conflicted, and emotionally scared. Many of these scars, which appear minor at first, leave major marks that can last a lifetime if unaddressed.

Those of us who are products of homes where intimacy was never publicly displayed, sometimes possess a greater longing for intimacy. As an adult, I struggled for years with longing for affirmation from women, in order to compensate for my lack of confidence. I was pretending that I did not need validation, while simultaneously craving it. I wanted to be admired for being so secure, camouflaging my insecurity by connecting sexually with women I crossed paths with. It was a challenge to understand that intimacy is not about connecting sexually, but about loving and understanding yourself before beginning a relationship. Many people have been used, abused, hurt or abandoned by those who said they loved us. But we're left with the residue of what we have been through, as well as the internal scars and bruises that we tend to cover up.

When I was about seven years old, I remember living in an apartment in South Los Angeles, California, with my mom and dad. My brothers and I often played in the street with the neighborhood kids until the street lights came on. I have memories of my mom walking me to Manchester Avenue Elementary School every day. On the steps of a local church located on the corner of 84th and Hoover, we shared an intimate moment that remains in my head as if it happened yesterday. Every day, regardless of how late we were or how many people were around, once we reached the steps of the church, she would look down at me and put one hand on her chin. She would not move until I put my hand on my chin. Then, we rocked back and forth, dancing, enjoying the time we shared from the apartment to the school. There was no music, only a shared understanding and enjoyment. As amazing as that experience was, that is one of the few intimate memories I remember sharing with my mother as a child. Although I had no idea about intimacy at that age, as an adult I now understand how experiences of the past, help to shape our understanding of intimacy.

My parents had five sons to raise alongside their struggles with drugs. Looking back, I can see that I failed to understand the severity of the situation since I was so young. I hadn't realized how much my brothers covered me from the truth about my parents and their drug use. My parents were led to the streets by their addiction and we found ourselves at home, alone for many days, with instructions to not open the door for anyone. One day while at home, my four brothers and I heard a knock on the front door. The temptation to open the door got the best of my older brother. He had no idea how drastically our lives would change once he opened the door. Social workers from the Department of Children and Family Services (DCFS) and the police charged in, placed the five of us in a car, and took us to a large room filled with many other kids in downtown Los Angeles, California. Without any words of wisdom to guide us or a family member to save us, we only had the fear that we were going to get in trouble for disobeying our parents. We had no clue about what was going on, but the experience of being taken away from our home, taken away from our parents, to be placed in foster care, definitely had its effect on all of us.

Sidenote:
Our experience with DCFS was not great, to say the least. However, the overall department is not bad and does great work to assist families in need.

After being in that room for a while, we thought we were going home once our parents came to pick us up, but we were wrong. That was one of the longest days of my life. It felt like a lifetime was spent in that room waiting. Later that evening, we were split up. My two eldest brothers went to one home and the youngest three found ourselves in another home. To this day, I have no clue how long we were in foster care. We were moved around from place to place with no explanation for what was happening.

Experiencing the negative stigma that comes with the foster care system, I remember longing for one more dance with my mom. When we finally settled at the third house, we still had no idea where our parents were or why they hadn't come to take us back home. After we were moved to the third house, it became really bad. Our temporary guardians treated us like the temporary residents that we were. I remember how we were literally forced to play in a backyard filled with fleas, day after day, overwhelmed by thoughts of not knowing if we were staying or leaving. I recall conversations being had about how it's better to just run away, then to stay with individuals who only wanted compensation and not the responsibility that comes with rearing three boys. Hopes of leaving or returning to our parents diminished as time passed, but salvation finally came.

On that day of redemption, my brothers and I headed outside to the backyard, the prison yard as we called it, as usual. While playing, we noticed a car pulling up to the side gate. We couldn't believe our eyes, but the sight of our grandmother getting out of that car was like a cold glass of ice water on a hot summer day. There are no words to describe how fast we ran to that gate. Although we were unable to go outside of the gate because it was locked, we were elated knowing that freedom was just on the other side. All three of us thought the same thing: finally, a familiar face has come to rescue us! After they loaded us in the car, we drove for about ten minutes. To our surprise, our two older brothers had been placed in a group home right around the corner from the home where we had been placed.

To this day, I thank God for my grandparents and will always be grateful that their love for us caused them to rescue us out of the foster care system. After raising their kids, my grandparents still determined that they would commit to raising the five Penn boys. They had a two-bedroom home, with five boys in one room while they slept in the other room. My grandmother was a strong-willed woman who adored cooking for the entire family, every Sunday. She lived what appeared a simple life before taking on this extra responsibility. As time passed, the more we began to understand that things were not so simple.

My grandfather was a hard-working man. He went to work at 6am, got off at 2pm, and would have to be back at the second job at 3pm. He didn't get home for the day until 11pm, sometimes even 12 in the morning. My grandmother also worked as a housekeeper for a motel near Los Angeles International Airport. After many years, she left her work and stayed at home to raise the five Penn boys. After taking in five young, active boys, things dramatically changed for my grandparents. They went from a household of two to a household of seven, based on their decision to not allow us to remain in the system. They were forced to move because the space was limited, so they found a three-bedroom home and we lived there for the next couple of years. Growing up with old school grandparents was interesting to say the least. Back then we were not asked if we wanted to go outside, we were told to go play in the front or the backyard; that was our only choice. That's funny because today, my kids stay in their rooms all day on their cell phones. I remember dinner consisted of all five boys at the table and Grandpa Jack eating wherever he could fit in.

Although they were married for over 20 years, I can't remember a time I saw them share an intimate moment, through words of affirmation, acts of service, quality time, gifts, or touch. At the age of eleven, my brothers and I started to observe how our grandparents would go to separate rooms at the end of the night. What appeared to be a loving and unified home suddenly displayed signs of distance and being disconnected. My grandmother was the strong, domineering partner in the relationship while my grandfather was passive aggressive. She made all the decisions and had the final say, if not the only say, regarding how things would go. Things appeared normal to those outside of our home. We regularly hosted family dinner on Sundays, giving the appearance of normalcy. As my brothers and I grew older, our curiosity heightened as we began to notice more. We noticed that our grandparents rarely talked to each other and, when they did, there was always an underlying negative tone. I cannot recall a time we saw them compliment each other, smile at the other or display any type of affection. After years of not seeing them be affectionate with each other, it became strange for us to see them interact without the usual exposition of my grandmother talking down to my grandfather. If they laughed together, it made us as happy as opening our gifts on Christmas Day! We rarely saw them in the same car together, and if they were, it would be to take us to a court appointment, giving the appearance of a perfect family. The older we became, the more we saw how unhappy our grandparents truly were. As unhappy as they were together, the unhappiness seemed multiplied since they felt they had to pretend when we were around. To this day, I have mixed feelings about them sacrificing their happiness in order to save us.

Sidenote:
Be careful about your reasons for sacrificing your happiness for the sake of others.

My grandfather had a wonderful personality, but life began to eat away at him as he found less happiness at home. When he came home after working all day, he sat in his car for hours before coming inside. In the evening, we would hear his car pull in the driveway. Curious to see if the current day would be different, I watched him from the bathroom window with the light off so he couldn't see me.

He would have this blank look on his face as he stared forward, looking at nothing except the deserted, empty, dark football field at Morningside High School. There was no music playing in the car; he just sat in silence. I could only wonder what was going through his mind as he sat there for hours. I looked as he stared emptily, unable to express himself, unable to walk in the home where he was paying rent, just to avoid arguing. Yes, he was physically at home, but we could see that his mind was in a completely different place.

Even as a young man, I started to resent my grandmother for treating my grandfather so unfairly. My grandparents had the appearance of a happy, married couple raising their grandsons when in actuality, intimacy was not the only thing they were missing. They were forced to remain in the same house for the sake of the Penn boys, despite their lack of love for one another. Soon, I found myself transferring my resentment towards women, in general, for the way my grandmother treated my grandfather.

There were many nights when I wanted to go out to the car and ask him what he was doing and what he was thinking about, but I was too afraid of my grandmother. This continued over the course of many years and it never got any better. The longer it lasted, the worse it became. It grew more difficult for my grandparents to talk civilly or hide how bad things really were.

When I was seventeen, I ran away from home. I found out later that my grandfather moved out of the house, although my grandparents never divorced. I desperately needed to understand my grandfather's perspective on intimacy. I had so many unanswered questions that I felt like I could have never asked as a young boy, so I was determined to find my grandfather.

After months of not knowing where he was, I finally found him not too far from where I was living. One day, I headed to his apartment and courageously knocked on the door, having played this conversation repeatedly in my head. I was finally ready to have a man-to-man talk with my grandfather regarding the impact his relationship had on my life.

When he opened the door and I saw how much weight he had lost and how much he aged since the last time I saw him, my courage dissipated. Our conversation was completely derailed as he began telling me that he was sick with cancer. The feeling I was left with was something I've lived with for many years, even after his passing.

How many times have you sacrificed, after finding out the truth, to spare the feelings of the person you cared about? Be honest! Too many times! There were so many things I learned from my grandfather, both good and bad. Two of those lessons that stand out are to work hard and to not be lazy.

After reflecting on my past relationships, I can unfortunately see how I also learned how to hide my feelings and cover up my pain. Growing up with my grandparents, watching how they interacted with each other, taught me a valuable principle— you can learn anything from anyone, including what not to do.

Sidenote:
Be careful what you tell others about yourself before understanding the truth behind the real reason.

Throughout the years of my previous marriage, I found myself doing the exact same thing as my grandfather, staying busy or staying outside the house until I had to go in — one of the downfalls of my marriage. I had gotten really good at holding my feelings and thoughts in until they began to impact external things. Not only was my attitude affected, my relationship with my children and my performance at work suffered because I could not stop pretending things were fine. The truth was, I was living a lie and, at any moment, I was ready to break. It wasn't until years later after talking to a dear friend that I realized that what I thought was the true reason for staying away from home, was not the reason at all.

Side note: Knowing the truth is so important. Take the time you need to acknowledge and deal with the truth of the past.

For years I thought I stayed away from home, when I was married, because my grandmother kept us in the house and did not allow us to go anywhere. I still struggle to remain still even now. I am often reminded of how my brothers and I were forced to remain home and play with only each other. We were not allowed to hang out with friends and friends were not allowed to come visit us. My grandmother was strict and refused to allow outside influences access to the home. It wasn't until after having children of my own, that I asked my grandmother why she was so strict. Her answer surprised me. All this time we thought she was just mean, when in reality she was operating out of fear. Her fear was that we would be hurt or killed in the streets. So, I began to think, what if your explanation for your actions is not the true reason at all?

CHAPTER

FIVE

"The first step toward change is awareness. The second step is acceptance."
Nathaniel Branden

WHAT IS YOUR TRUTH?

How much of what you've gone through has impacted your ability to establish or maintain relationship? Although being taken away from my parents at the age of seven took its toll on my brothers and me, I was fortunate to have conversations regarding my childhood with my mother before her passing. It took many years for me to forgive my parents for their neglect and abandonment.

I forgave my mom first, but it took a few more years to forgive my dad. Because I chose to forgive, I am now able to recognize past intimate moments

Sidenote: Forgiveness is crucial when trying to move forward. It's hard to develop anything when the foundation is unstable.

shared with my parents, including conversations about the hurt in my past. Those conversations helped me to see why they made the choices they did, like using drugs, which led to us being taken away. During one of those conversations, I vividly remember the hurt and disappointment plastered on my mom's face recalling how DCFS received an anonymous phone call that informed them of five minors that were left alone with no supervision. I thought it was over, but as I reminisced, all the hurt from my childhood resurfaced as I described to my mom all the pain that resulted from their actions. I was extremely emotional recalling the day we answered that unforgettable knock at the door, only to have law enforcement take us away. I had spent years trying to suppress that memory. When we were placed in the foster care system, we were too young to understand why our parents had not come to pick us up. It took me years to admit that those memories from the past left numerous scars. Now, I see how these scars impacted my ability to trust women. It became evident that when issues of yesterday go unresolved, it only leads to further disappointment. For example, my parents abandoning us ended with us being raised by our grandparents. Ironically enough, it took years of counseling to realize that the reason we placed so much blame on our mom and grandmother was because they were the first two women role models that shaped our thoughts about love, family, intimacy and pain.

We were raised by our paternal grandmother who did not care for our mother. Throughout our childhood, our grandmother continually fed us negative thoughts about our mother. She believed everything that happened was my mother's fault. I've since gained a greater appreciation for my mom and the things I went through as a child. I understand that she loved us as best as she could, then and up until her death.

I come from a broken home. My parents were on drugs, my brothers and I were in foster care, I ran away from home and had a baby at 17 years old, that is my truth. The past does not simply go away. What is your truth?

You are who you are, but this comes with the truth of knowing from where you come and coming to peace with it. What is the real truth? Sometimes, we learn from our parents' mistakes. Some of us know how to give what we never had or know how to love like we were never loved. But *Intimacy Beyond the Bedroom* is not something you observe and simply pick up. There are times when we experience things, but don't admit it because the truth hurts. Acknowledging where you are in life is a choice that can be a hard reality. This is especially difficult when you see others who have companions, but they've compromised their values, goals, and even their personality to get what they have. What is your truth? Come on, it's time to be honest! Even if you are longing for *Intimacy Beyond the Bedroom* you need to refuse to settle for just anybody and anything. Refuse to waste time with people when you know that there is no authentic reciprocity.

Side note: Regardless of the experience, you're blessed to have (or have had) the parents God gave you.

Admitting your truth will often force you to deal with the question, "Why am I alone?" Knowing your truth, and owning the fact that something about you is different, will keep you from settling for anything less than what you deserve. It's your truth, so own it.

Intimacy Beyond the Bedroom is something that's not only craved when you are single, but it can also be lacking in your relationships. This is because most people have an ideal fantasy but still won't admit their truth. What others enjoy in their singleness or in their relationships may not be what works for you and yours.

Intimacy Beyond the Bedroom recognizes the fact that there isn't a one size fits all solution when it comes to the desire for and fulfillment of intimacy. When you live your truth, people may think something is wrong with you. People may judge you based on what they can see externally, without knowing the space you're in and how you got there. If you wanted to be with just anyone, you could. But settling for just anybody won't work. The bottom line is: don't allow the pressure of the way things appear to dictate what you know to be true. Don't let someone else's opinion today jeopardize your tomorrow. Remember, possibilities are endless if you believe it.

CHAPTER

SIX

*"Truth and facts are woven together.
However, sometimes facts can blind
you from seeing what is actually going
on in someone's life."*
Shannon L. Alder

THE POWER OF PRESENTATION

How many times have you covered up, held yourself back, or simply refused to expose yourself to someone because of what you've been through in your past? What you see is not always what you get. Looks and feelings are very deceiving especially when it comes to intimacy. How many times have you settled for a single moment, whether it was a kiss, sex, or a hug, only to be left feeling empty and your needs unmet? Hopefully enough to not settle any longer! I remember going on many dates, and having sex with women, fully knowing there was no future because I lacked a true understanding of intimacy. People who are unhappy internally sometimes fill their time with other people, in order to avoid having to spend time alone. During my dating phase, even though there appeared to be a mutual understanding, eventually they wanted more from me than I was able or willing to give. Just because a person satisfies you, doesn't mean that they're fulfilling your longing or your greatest desire.

A person can give you something without much thought behind how it will impact you later on. Here is a reality check: just because a person has sex with you doesn't mean they have been intimate with you! There have been times when I've had sex with a woman and didn't have a moment of intimacy. There were times when I would be willing to open her legs, but refused to open my heart. Engaging in sex only made me feel better for the moment.

Sidenote:
Temporary satisfaction is far from fulfillment.

Even after being married for ten years, I could see the similarities between mine and my grandparent's marriage. Many stay in relationships to avoid facing the hard reality that it's not going to work. Relationships don't end because of infidelity only. The fact is you can be in a relationship and not be committed to it. For instance, after the divorce, I had several sexual relationships. What's interesting is that my partners and I had different perspectives regarding the same event. We were in the same room, engaged in the same act, but on two totally different pages regarding the relationship. Can you remember a time, while in the heat of the moment of a sexual encounter, desiring to feel loved instead? Have you ever experienced a physical encounter (kiss, hug, a dance, a look) with someone, but it missed everything that comes with intimacy?

Here's a more important question to ponder: how can you be in love with a person you don't really know? I know that "make love" sounds deeper than "let's have sex," so we say it to feel better about the action. The truth is, there are times when people want something superficial and it's no deeper than that.

Intimacy Beyond the Bedroom is not about a lack of sex. It's about having a deeper awareness of self first, then allowing the other person the privilege of knowing the real you outside of sex. For example, in my previous marriage, it wasn't because I didn't know what she liked in the bedroom that caused us to lack intimacy, it was because we both had unmet needs beyond the bedroom. For some it's easy to ignore difficulties in your relationship by being physical, but for others how things are outside of the bedroom will impact the way things are in the bedroom. Perspective.

The quality of any relationship is directly related to the effort put in. The energy and effort you put into a thing directly impacts the outcome. Therefore, the quality of your relationship is directly related to the effort both parties put in. The intimacy enjoyed in a relationship will be the result of both individuals' effort. Some people fail to understand true intimacy simply because we miss that it must start with an understanding of self. How many times have we complained that a person doesn't meet a need and you feel unfulfilled in the relationship? Although the desire could be felt physically, the greater need for intimacy rears its head as a longing that goes deeper than physical satisfaction. *Intimacy Beyond the Bedroom* primarily focuses on you as an individual, and less on the other person. Although the end goal should be fulfillment, the process by which we attain it cannot be overlooked. It involves learning about ourselves in order to root out selfishness and to also provide a better understanding to our partner. When you fail to root out selfishness, your motives are based on what you need to do to ensure you get what you want from the relationship rather than focusing on how do we fulfill one another's needs. I can recall in my previous marriage where we would go without speaking to one another for weeks. We would talk in passing, but that's not really communicating nor is it an atmosphere for intimacy. We behaved this way because *Intimacy Beyond the Bedroom* was foreign to us. Sex became self-serving, happening only after weeks of built-up tension. One of us would ask the other for sex like we were asking to borrow money from a friend.

As long as we continued to go through the motions of presenting one thing and doing something entirely different, the less intimacy we shared with each other. Birthdays, holidays, Mother's Day and Father's Day began to be acknowledged out of obligation to each other rather than appreciation and love. Obligation says, "I have to," when motivation says, "I want to." Just because people stay together does not mean that what they "present to the public" is true. It's not just about knowing the truth, we have to be willing to accept it, learn why it's true and decide how to change it so it's the truth we want to see. Problems can't be resolved without acknowledging that there is a problem. We often fall for people who present themselves as if they're a well-rounded individual, but they lack follow through and consistency. We judge from

Side note:
You cannot share intimate moments with a person without connectivity.

outward appearances, without considering if it is worth waiting and learning about who the individual really is. Often, we fall for individuals simply by observing them, only to find that after you've made a commitment, their presentation was a show.

As a man, I look back at numerous times where I was selfish and self-centered. There were times I caused damage to others, without realizing the severity, because I didn't know how damaged I really was. Regardless of the reason, it's important for me to apologize to women I've hurt now that I truly understand that hurt people, hurt people. Ladies, I apologize and sincerely ask for your forgiveness.

CHAPTER

SEVEN

"With relationships comes access,
and with intimacy comes
influence."
Tommy Tenney

ACCESS GRANTED

How much time do you allow yourself to be alone in between seasons of your life before granting access to the next person? Osho, a philosopher and mystic states, "No relationship can truly grow if you go on holding back. If you remain clever and go on safeguarding and protecting yourself, only personalities meet, and the essential centers remain alone."

After my divorce, and before I remarried, I can remember meeting women who I thought had great potential, but I would only let them in so far. As wonderful as the time spent was, there was something deeper missing that I had yet to personally achieve. It wouldn't allow me to fully commit. Although these were beautiful, intelligent, accomplished and financially stable women, there was still something significant missing. It was not until I took an honest assessment of myself, that I finally understood the missing piece was not someone, but me making a decision to really commit. So, when my relationship reached a place of the possibility of marriage, I started to really assess things honestly.

Here are some important questions I asked myself that will help you assess if you should move forward in your relationship or if you should redirect:

- Is it a great fit?

- Would either of us compromise who we are if we decided to be together?

- Does the reason you want to be with this person surpass their looks and intelligence?

- Are they good for you and not only good to you? Likewise, are you right for them?

- If you move forward with them, do you feel you're leaving your best life behind or can you foresee better days ahead?

- What is their family dynamic?

Did you answer the questions honestly? These questions may not seem important to some, and might seem superficial to others, but they may help someone pivot rather than invest in a lie.

It's interesting now how the world is being forced to wear masks to protect us from the Coronavirus. That outward mask is symbolic to the emotional, mental, and physical mask most of us wore prior to the pandemic. I did not want to acknowledge to myself, or admit to anyone else, that I was wearing a mask. Whenever we hide behind these masks and avoid operating in the truth, relationships can only last so long.

When we wear masks, there are four people in the relationship, not two. Two pretenders go on engaging, and the two real people remain worlds apart. I spent years engaging in surface-level relationships with individuals as the pretender. Most won't acknowledge it, but when you're negatively impacted by your past and avoid taking the needed time to heal, you end up becoming an imposter in your relationships. We pretend to be ready to date, when we're not. We pretend to be open, when we really are not open to trusting. We pretend to understand the work involved, when we really don't want to commit to doing the work necessary to experience intimacy.

Side note: As much as we would like to, we can't give others the keys to doors that we have yet to access ourselves.

I went through years of dating, getting married, getting divorced, and dating again, only to realize that I was intentionally blocking my feelings. I prevented myself from getting close to anyone to avoid the possibility of getting hurt again. In reality, it was the fear of failure that prevented me from allowing others to access my true self.

In my past experiences, I attempted to develop friendships and relationships without taking the needed time to heal and reflect. Much of my desire for companionship eclipsed the reality that I would continue to fail if I didn't change. I was repeating mistakes because I failed to take the time to access the part of me that I intentionally ignored for years — the hurt, low self-esteem, insecurity, and dishonesty. In retrospect, failing to understand who I was perpetuated a cycle that prevented me from developing feelings and committing to others. I intentionally kept this door locked because I didn't want to deal with what was truly behind it. I'm not proud of it, but one of the things I learned as a result of my childhood was how to pretend things didn't bother me, even when it did. I became a professional at hiding my true feelings and wearing that aforementioned mask. When it came to love, I allowed access to my representative, and not my true person who I had yet to know for myself. Year after year, many of us go through cycles of establishing physical connections and granting access to individuals who, if we were to be honest, would not stand a chance with us today if we knew then what we know now.

While reflecting on past relationships, I can only imagine the damage, disappointment, and hurt that I caused others because I was hurt myself. I found myself damaging people because I was unwilling to accept that, even if I wanted a companion, inner healing proved to be a necessary and difficult task. My lack of commitment and fear of rejection oftentimes caused me to shut others out to avoid having to answer for my own inadequacies. Who we are and what we do is influenced by what we've experienced. I denied women access to my true self, but I did not understand at the time where that behavior originated. Fear is crippling, and sometimes uncontrollable, unless we're willing to face it. During my previous marriage, I was intent on proving that I was mature enough for the commitment marriage required. Regrettably, I was not mature enough to acknowledge that marriage is a huge step, believing everything I needed to know would easily be learned over time. I only allowed partial access to the real me, assuming it would be easier to deal with my fears and insecurities having someone next to me, rather than sorting through it alone. I was wrong.

What I thought was for the best ended up being a life changing mistake. The pain of divorce could've been avoided if I had just taken the time to examine myself before making that lifelong commitment. Before we allow someone access, we need to be honest about what truly resides behind the doors of our hearts and minds. Taking the time for self-reflection gives us the time we need to deal with past pain, disappointment, and unfulfilled desires that continue to guide our decisions.

Granting access doesn't just deal with allowing others in, but rather allowing yourself the time and space needed to access the real you. Access granted means we acknowledge our issues before seeking fulfillment from others, opening the door for new relationships. It's amazing how often we suppress our true needs and appear to be ready for a relationship and marriage, while we neglect the important principle that teaches us to, "love others as you love yourself." Failing to love myself resulted in my failure to love others the right way. The more time I spent taking an introspective look at myself, the more I discovered that I not only kept others out, but even greater, I denied access to myself. That access includes acknowledging the pain of my childhood abandonment issues, the hurt caused by individuals who said they loved me but their actions reflected something different, and simply dealing with how all those things impacted my thoughts and actions.

I realized that all this time, I continually ignored and hid who I was, which caused feelings of inadequacy as a father, husband, friend, brother and, most importantly, a man. When I finally acknowledged the truth, I was not afraid to address issues in my past that had impacted me so deeply. So many people are afraid to admit to themselves how much of what has happened to them in the past still affects them. Additionally, we don't like to admit our past to other people because we don't like revisiting the truth ourselves. The truth of the matter is that your situation did happen and if you ignore that truth, it will continue to have a negative impact on you. In fact, people who have been hurt will sooner or later hurt other people, if their pain goes unaddressed. Joyce Meyer, author and Bible teacher, says it best: "hurt people, hurt people." Thus, we will continue to pass on years of pain and hurt to others if we refuse to admit and address unresolved issues of the past.

I recall making minor issues a major deal in order to deny access to people who wanted to spend time with me. I denied them access because I was secretly struggling to find my own self-worth. I only kept people around to fill a void, not because they gained access. I would spend time with women even when there was no future. There were women who I cared for, but I knew that friendship was all we would have. I refused anything that would cause me to commit to another person, even if those same individuals may have seen a future with me. Once I was dating a woman and I remember how amazing our time was together, even without sex. She made everything seem like it would be fine when we were around each other. We laughed, experienced times of sorrow, we shared success and failures, we both loved God, and we spent a lot of time with each other. I finally realized, however, that although things were going great, I was making her miss out on time with the person for whom she was meant. I had to be honest with her, and with myself, and end the relationship.

Sidenote: Just because someone is at the door of your life doesn't mean you have to grant access and just because you have someone doesn't mean they're the right person for you.

When we are lonely, we are more inclined to begin a relationship just to have someone there to fill the space, rather than wait for the right person at the right time. Have you ever given someone access or stayed with someone who you knew was not meant to stay with you forever? Have you wanted so desperately for them to be the right one that you invested your time and heart only to find that it still didn't work? It's those moments that help us discover our truth. Access granted is less about a person and more about learning you and knowing what comes with being you.

We can spend years with a person without being granted access to who they truly are. Many times we ignore the truth and start to conform into what the person we have allowed access to wants. There's always another side to the story, the side that can't be seen simply by observation. Rather, one has to be granted access to know the real truth.

When my wife and I were dating, we would arrange a time for her to come over after work. Before giving her a key to my apartment, she would call when she arrived. This went on for almost a year, me having to unlock the door to allow her access. This particular day, we had planned for her to come over a little earlier and she asked if I was going to leave the door open for her.

Side note:
Not only are there always two sides to a story, but oftentimes your side may not be the real truth.

After I thought about it, I replied, "not only the physical door, but the door to my heart is open." It sounds like a pickup line, but I was attempting to express my openness to her having access in my life.

It is astonishing how many people we allow to come around, but we still don't let them in. Access granted is not about your ability to find love, it's about your ability to unlock the compartments of your life that contain all the valuable experiences that have made you who you are. Access granted has to do with valuing yourself enough to be okay with the quality of people you have around, rather than the quantity. Too many times we keep ourselves closed off around people because we are private or because we don't easily trust. Before we move any further, let's have a moment of truth. Is that your true reason for closing yourself off or is it an excuse at this point? How much of where you are now has to do with you alone?

CHAPTER EIGHT

"I am not a day dreamer, I am a believer, that after every painful love I have gone through, it is just an experience to crack open the deepest parts of my core and allow to me to delve into a passion so rare, that I will find a love that was almost, never meant to be."
Nikki Rowe

FINDERS KEEPERS

How many moments in the past have caused you to say, "I'm looking for someone who has the power to deal with the real me?" Vishwas Chavan, Author & Founder of the School of Inspirational Living, asserts that, "Once you achieve self-intimacy & self-connection, success, peace and wealth [are] not far from you." When I became a man, I told myself that I was going to find a woman who would treat me differently than the way my grandmother treated my grandfather. My mindset was so extreme, that if a woman appeared strong-willed and very opinionated, there was little to no attraction for me. I refused to become the person I remembered my grandfather was forced to become — a person unhappy with life. I made every attempt to prevent even the slightest notion that a woman was controlling me.

Most men postulate that their number one need in a relationship is respect, but for me it is an extremely strict requirement. My need for respect was so strong that when I found a woman who appeared to fit what I imagined, and one that I felt truly respected me, I automatically assumed that I found the right individual with whom I was going to spend my life. I missed the fact that there were other significant aspects to a relationship that I was missing as well. I acknowledged all the things I wanted to see and ignored multiple warning signs.

For example, after my first marriage, I was with a woman who was very helpful. She served even to the point where she would prioritize serving others before considering me, her date. Despite her being very catering, I willfully ignored any drawbacks I saw; I did not want to admit them. She struggled to be honest about her true feelings when confronted because she wanted to be liked by everyone. Even when asked how she felt, she would find it hard to take a stance and she was very passive-aggressive. When she wanted to say "no" to things, she would find herself agreeing or saying "yes," regardless of how it made her feel and regardless if she and I already had an understanding on the issue. Her focus was solely on how she was perceived by others.

I can remember a time she and I were out and another man approached her. He asked her if he could buy her a drink and, instead of her declining because we were on a date, she took the drink to not appear "rude." Her placement in the "friend zone" was immediate at that point. As the night progressed, I couldn't wait for the date to end. The next night she asked to go out again. I was honest with her and told her how her actions made me feel. I thought I'd found someone who could possibly meet my needs, but I was mistaken.

Needless to say, there is no perfect person; there

is only the person we believe is worth our time and attention. I remember thinking how I could not wait to start over and begin rebuilding the things that were torn down after my divorce. It wasn't too long after being single again that I decided to stop looking for the right person, and began the process of finding the true me. Teaching myself to not look for *Intimacy Beyond the Bedroom* in others was not as simple as it sounds. I had to take the responsibility I placed on others and place the ownership back on myself.

"Finders keepers" is about discovering your truth and finding someone who not only fits you, but also about finding the person who understands the work it takes to release the greatness that's on the inside of you. This is the person who possesses the patience and understanding about what you can be before you GROW there. This is the person who wants to deal with the real you. The part of you that may not be perfect but the part that is on the road to greatness. This act of becoming whole, or riding into your greatness, means that you might not be healed from everything in your past, but you recognize the work it will take to heal from the pain, buried on the inside, and that you commit to doing it.

Once we find those lingering hurts that hide within us, we must be willing to do the work to resolve them. After that, the true pursuit of happiness can begin and can be fully enjoyed. It allows us to move away from pretending and showing people a fake version of ourselves to a place of being happy about discovering what makes us who we really are. We often desire immediate results that only come after we go through the process; I call it the microwave syndrome. This process allows us time to reflect and assess our experiences in order to uncover the truth. We need to realize how significant the "going through" process is in relation to finding and owning our truth. Once you discover the real you, it's worth keeping and protecting at all costs. I often wonder how many of us really know who we are and what we really need versus the things we want from someone else?

Side note:
You say you want a strong person, but beware. While a person may have qualities that appear strong on the outside, that doesn't mean you have found an individual who is strong enough to support where you are.

We deceive ourselves when we base our relationship decisions off outward appearances only. Just because a person is wearing glasses doesn't mean they have a high IQ, likewise never judge a book by its cover. Value has to be found in the process of understanding yourself first; finding out who you really are and owning it. You have to own it to the point of not allowing your desire for companionship to cause you to compromise your values, losing what took you time to find.

Many times, people introduce their "representative" as the person they want other people to see. A liar will not introduce himself as a liar, nor would a manipulator or someone who is damaged. Initially, most people have a version of themselves that they introduce to others who is void of flaws and almost perfect. Other times, we base the version of ourselves we introduce to others on the dynamics of that relationship. Depending on the level of attraction, that determines the presentation we give. If we need to be more intelligent, we adjust the way we speak. If we are meeting a person who is "healthy," we tend to present ourselves as a "gym rat" who eats well. However, the truth is, if it is not a good fit, it's simply not a good fit. Not being our true selves and not being genuine is like going to a doctor, not telling them the real symptoms and expecting them to provide an accurate diagnosis. We don't realize that starting off a relationship with lies will only yield more lies, more deception, and less acknowledgment of the truth. We don't realize that the truth is what gives us the freedom to be our real selves.

How can we expect other people to be real with us if we're not willing to be real with ourselves? We can't! What happens when two people introduce themselves as the person they would like to be instead of who they truly are? At times we fall for a person's "representative" and not the real individual. Therefore, *Intimacy Beyond the Bedroom* has to be seen as a necessity and not an option. It should be understood by both parties individually and should come after understanding the difference between satisfaction and fulfillment.

"Finders keepers" has everything to do with discovering the truth in ourselves and others, which can lead to a life of happiness when we proceed with caution. It's not only the end result that matters, but it's the process by which the end result is achieved. The road to understanding *Intimacy Beyond the Bedroom* is not one size fits all. It does not happen overnight, nor does it manifest itself without real effort. What may be intimacy to one does not necessarily equate to intimacy for another. Many of us enter the next relationship with a person the same way we exit the past relationships, yet wonder why we end up with the same results. The reason is because we lack a true understanding of intimacy. Judging from the outside appearance is a repeated mistake that causes many people to get derailed. We see what might be wonderful potential and we immediately figure it must be the thing we desired but what you see is not always what you get.

There's a great lesson I learned not too long ago — the difference between a reveal date and a release date. Many times, before a product is released to the general public, there is a reveal date. The reveal date indicates that a new product will be released soon, building anticipation before the actual launch date. During a reveal date, we get to see the product, and possibly demo it before we have the option of purchasing it. The reveal date is only to demonstrate what is to come down the line. Seeing it increases our excitement and expectations, but we can't do much at the reveal date, except wait. We wait in lines and we even check to see if the release date has moved up, for the potential to get the product earlier than the expected date. We are only able to possess it if we're willing to go where we need to go; no exceptions. Just think, many people are willing to wait in a line to spend over one thousand dollars to buy a phone, but fail to acquire the skills necessary to effectively communicate with their partner. In "finders keepers," we sometimes find someone who we thought was a keeper and let them in too soon. We reveal too much without the understanding that timing is everything and we may want to hold out until the actual release.

After years of living single, dating without a purpose, and thinking marriage was no longer an option I wanted, I found myself getting married again. Although I believed marriage was not a desire I cared to entertain again, meeting my wife, Quiana, was effortless. Let me say, sometimes you meet your person when you're not looking for them. The day we met was a normal day filled with responsibilities, like every other week. I recall how emotionally drained I was that day. I was so drained that a friend refused to let me sit in the house another minute without taking some much-needed time for myself. It is times like the aforementioned when it is important to have the right individuals around you, who know the real you enough to know when you're not yourself.

A mutual friend was having a birthday party on a night neither of us wanted to be out. Quiana was forced to come to this party by her sister, who wanted to help get her mind off her previous marriage anniversary. I was forced to take a ride with a friend, to get some much-needed fresh air after a long, emotionally draining day. As she tells the story, we

Side note:
There are people who will wait in line overnight for expensive shoes, yet refuse to go the extra mile for the person they claim to love.

arrived at the same time since they were parked right behind my car. I believe she sought after me from the very beginning, even though she would never admit it.

I walked into the party, took my position on the wall so I could people watch, as usual. After a while, Quiana, her sister, and another friend walked over and stood near where I was standing. At first neither of us made eye contact and neither showed any interest in the other, but somehow we ended up standing next to each other. Ironically enough, our meeting wasn't as romantic as you would think. Her sister asked my friend to hold her drink while she went to the restroom. My friend, who could not hold her drink, handed me the drink, which was aggressively impeded by Quiana, a Sergeant with the Sheriff's Department. I want to emphasize the aggressiveness by which she stepped in to take her sister's drink. She thought that we may be part of some sort of a date rape drug ring. My initial response to her was that I never asked to hold the drink and secondly, I didn't care that she didn't want me to hold her sister's drink. I continued to observe the room and people watched. That moment, as crazy as it was, turned out to be our first impressions of one another. Even to this day, we laugh — and disagree — about exactly how we came to meet each other. We are constantly in awe of the way things worked out; finding each other at a time and place which neither of us expected. But we are both grateful that we went to the party that day.

Getting to know my wife and allowing her to get to know me, proved to be a challenge. This was a challenge which she welcomed, and feared. She had an uncanny ability to penetrate the walls of defense around my heart; her willingness to be honest, her confidence and determination were like no other. As fast as she wanted things to go, I understood the importance of things moving at the right pace. The right time is just as important as finding the right person. Understanding timing will either increase or decrease the amount of struggle and enjoyment one will experience in their relationship. It is very possible to meet the wrong person at the right time (you may be ready and available for a relationship, but they're unavailable) and, even, the right person at the wrong time (you may meet a person who is available for a relationship, but you're still not healed or maybe just getting out of a relationship).

As we started to build our relationship, I was honest with her regarding my feelings towards marriage at the time, as was she. Although I had been divorced for longer than she had, I didn't think I would be getting married again before the age of 50. We both agreed that we didn't want any more kids since we both have three beautiful girls of our own. Early on, I told her that for me to be in another relationship, I would have to desire to be around that person more than I enjoyed my single life. *Intimacy Beyond the Bedroom* is not about sex, money, or what someone else could do for you. Yet, many people feel that after they get married, they have to sacrifice their previous life. I refused to move forward thinking that I would lose my best life in order to find her. One of our goals in our relationship was to spend time finding out more about each other and learning our likes and dislikes, past struggles, our failures and understanding how we

Side note: Your ability to move forward, will be impacted when there's regret about the past.

think. It was a welcomed challenge for both of us.

One specific area regarding "finders keepers" deals with the fact that at times, we all have some sort of wall up that keeps people out of our heart and keeps our true feelings in. I've learned that much of what I was doing dealt with the fact that I was not trying to keep people out, but wanting the right person to find their way past the surface, to the heart of who I really was. People have a bad habit of making others feel badly for wanting their partner to learn how to keep them. "Finders keepers" is an encouragement to not allow yourself to be put off if it takes you longer to share yourself with someone.

"Finders keepers" is about you owning your own value while in the process of finding a mate. As much as we may feel that we are ready, most of us only feel the need for companionship. We don't truly understand the importance of allowing ourselves to be true to ourselves, rather than what others have deemed important or unimportant. Once you find yourself, own it, protect it, and refuse to compromise based on what looks and feels good. "Finders keepers" is for those who understand their worth, know the value they bring, and unapologetically walk with self-awareness, even if that means being alone until that right person comes. The key to unlocking the true you should not be given away hastily. It should be treasured

Sidenote:
It's not easy being vulnerable when you've had to learn to protect yourself from letdown, hurt, and disappointment.

and treated with care. It has to be found and owned

first, by you as the owner, then searched for and appreciated by the person who doesn't mind putting in the work to find it.

CHAPTER NINE

"Recognizing isn't at all like seeing; the two often don't even agree."
Sten Nadolny

THINGS ARE NOT ALWAYS
WHAT THEY SEEM

How many times have you judged a book by its cover, only to find out that it was not what you thought it was? In my previous marriage, I realized that I desired much more, so after the divorce, I began to seek the truth about what I truly needed. I spent time with women who seemed one way, but after some time, my needs were still unmet. When I met Quiana, I had a renewed mindset and knew what I needed.

We often make the mistake of assuming that if something looks or feels good, it automatically means that it will be good. We struggle to see that what we want and need is often a great distance from each other. For me, I often struggled between my reality and what I wanted to be, simply because I was operating in my emotions and not the truth. Oftentimes, my perspective about the present was obscured by a false perception of a situation that was based on my desire.

To this day, I enjoy observing how different couples interact with one another in public, and other various settings. I enjoy seeing how they communicate and how they display their affection. It wasn't until later in my previous marriage that I realized just how unhappy we were and how long we pretended things were okay. During our last years of marriage, we were far from happy. I was too disappointed in our reality to admit it to myself and too embarrassed to tell others the truth. Just because we talked in public didn't mean that we communicated in private. There were times we talked, but we struggled to understand each other. We went to events, even attended church, and pretended to be on the same page. But deep down inside, we did not want people to know that we were broken and in need of more than what we were willing to give each other. People would observe what appeared to be a healthy relationship, but had no clue that we were simply pretending we had it all together to avoid scrutiny.

We both felt alone, desperate, and unwanted. Five years into our marriage, this sad existence became our new norm; it hurt to admit. As I look back, the ironic thing is that I became a specialist at helping others fix their relationships, all while covering up the deficiencies in my own. I spent years helping others become better in areas where I lacked the willingness to address similar issues. I spent years trying to cover up my insufficiencies, attempting to divert attention away from anything that would make my relationship look unhealthy.

It wasn't until the last two years of that marriage, the early stages of the divorce, that I was able to deal with the things that were going on inside of me and in the marriage. As tough as it was, it was only after much deep self-reflection that I truly began to understand how badly I needed to heal. After admitting that these issues resided inside of me, I realized that my actions and my behaviors were a true reflection of the inner me. I was ashamed to admit that the counseling I provided to others was not working for my own marriage and that I was facing the same issues as the people I helped. It got to the point that I became numb. I pretended to be someone else on the outside, hiding the real issues that lurked on the inside. If asked to describe my personality, people would say I was confident, outgoing, jovial, and even arrogant at times. I was a master at adapting to my situation and hiding my deep-rooted issues. It got to the point where I tailored my actions based on what people assumed. I thought that if they presumed I was confident and happy, then my issues were probably not as bad as I thought.

What I felt on the inside (my ex-wife and I were simply not meant for each other) was a feeling that many people advised me not to give in to. Eventually, I had to realize what I stated earlier —- not only does the truth make us free, but it also gives us the freedom to be true to our real selves and to experience true peace. During those years, I asked myself repeatedly what would happen if I allowed myself to be true to who I was, rather than being who other people told me I needed to be, if I wanted to be accepted and loved? How could I honestly help others when I was living a lie? Sometimes the more we're honest with ourselves, the more we find ourselves alone.

While I was married, I remember days and nights when my daughters and my ex-wife were there, but I felt so lonely and unappreciated. This was not because of something they had done to me, but because I failed to deal with the battle in my mind about the type of intimacy I longed for. Like other families, we played games and my daughters cheated, although they deny it even to this day. Like other families, we went to the movies and would go out for dinner. To the outside world, those moments gave the appearance that everything in our family was normal. Indeed, those were some great moments, but as great as those moments were, there were still unresolved issues within me. We enjoyed having fun with each other, but I could not own up to the harsh reality that those temporary moments covered up times where conversations should have taken place. Open and honest communication is a necessity when attempting to work through underlying issues in a relationship. As I look back, I realize that my ex-wife and I struggled to move past the appearance of how things looked as opposed to actually doing the work to reach a place of true resolution.

During our ninth year of marriage, we had a conversation where we finally admitted how we never reached a place of truly being on the same page with one another. As much as we wanted to, we never got to the place where most couples determine that no matter what, they will make it through the tough times. We simply lacked that determination. After the divorce, I lived alone, and I still dealt with cravings for *Intimacy Beyond the Bedroom*. Experience has a way of teaching us lessons the hard way, in order to grow the right way. After experiencing divorce, I had to learn how to closely evaluate the character of a person versus what I saw on the outside. Going off appearance will cause you to be in a rush to start a relationship, leading to a broken heart and a bruised ego all over again. It took years for me to realize the importance of consistency over time.

Some men and women have a problem revealing their true selves in the beginning of a relationship, for various reasons. However, it is not easy to maintain an image if you are pretending to be someone who you are not. The point here is things are not always what they appear, but

Side note: If you can't maintain a characteristic, you shouldn't even bother introducing it to someone.

when they do appear, how you respond will determine what you should expect.

CHAPTER

TEN

"I know now: what is, is all that matters.
Not the thing you know is meant to be, not
what could be, not what should be, not what
ought to be, not what once was.
Only the is."
Augusten Burroughs

TO BE OR NOT TO BE

How many of us have changed our desires based on what we have experienced? After going through many life challenges and after many mistakes, I found myself spending time with all types of people with different backgrounds. I went places and did things in an attempt to fill a void in my life. I went through the motions of having fun even though I constantly questioned myself and my purpose. I was waiting for someone to tell me that despite my actions, I was much better than what I was going through. With all the people around, I remember individuals repeatedly asking what I needed, but my reply was always, "I'm good."

Another tough lesson that I learned through marriage and life after divorce was that *Intimacy Beyond the Bedroom* does not start with the external; it should start with an internal understanding of oneself. One has to know his

Side note:
How can we tell someone what we need when we have yet to understand what we need ourselves?

or herself before they can truly understand and appreciate sharing intimacy with another person. Time and time again, after repeated frustration, and after ending many temporary connections, I started to understand how important valuing me is when it comes to intimacy. Each connection I had with others appeared to be my chance at a promising future, yet I continued in the same cycle of starting and ending. I struggled to commit to relationships that showed promise after my divorce because I didn't want to, "put all of my eggs in one basket." Even when I met women who seemed ready for a lasting relationship, I only gave so much of myself and intentionally sabotaged the relationship. Eventually, I forced myself into a space in which I had to take time to ask myself is my desire, "to be or not to be?"

Based on the continual cycle, it made me wonder. Have I ever truly experienced intimacy? Why do I attract the wrong people? Why do I continually entertain people who I know are not fulfilling? The search for answers to these questions helped me realize that I had grown accustomed to temporary satisfaction. That temporary feeling outweighed my desire to be fulfilled. The problem was not the individuals I attracted; the problem was the value I placed on myself. Have you ever felt as if you "checked all the boxes," but still wondered what was wrong with you? When you find your "to be," you don't need to check all the boxes, you need to check the right box.

Questioning your "to be or not to be" intensifies most often because of an unfulfilled desire. Those desires have to do with things we experienced in our past, what we're experiencing in the present, and what we want to experience in the future. Desires that cause us to deal with where we think we should be or how we think things should be, start to consume our thoughts. We try to either do better than the bad examples before us or we settle for something in an effort to avoid being left with nothing. Regardless of the relationship, whether a marriage, friendship, or partnership, you can't make what's meant "to be" happen by attaching yourself to just anyone. Much of what we want may not come to be according to the timeline we have set. At times we set goals and milestones for ourselves that we often end up altering later. Have you ever felt like a failure because you didn't meet your timeline? This is not because of someone else, but it is primarily because of the INNER ME. Some people say they want to be married by 30 and if they're not, they feel like a failure. But, would you rather have met the goal of marriage by 30 only to turn around and get divorced at 35 or meet your "to be" in your fifties and live happily married for the next forty years?

After many mistakes, life has taught me, the hard way, how some of the painful things I'd experienced could have been avoided if my maturity matched my expectations. I often thought that it would have been better if the women I dated would've come at a time when I was better prepared to handle the responsibility that comes with having a relationship. Now, it seems easy to be able to say I wasn't ready to date, but it was hard to admit that at that time. Can you imagine the hurt that would've been avoided in the past had you and the other person been honest with each other from the beginning?

Your "to be or not to be" is an internal dilemma that may appear to leave you feeling left out because of your determination to be where you envisioned yourself. On the contrary, there are individuals who do not know how to be alone, and are not happy themselves, so they settle for anyone to come along and fill a space. I was one of those people! Many of us spend years repeating certain behaviors and characteristics and we do not even realize how much our behaviors reflect how we think.

There were times when I intentionally distanced myself from people because I was afraid of someone discovering my truth. As much as we try to conceal the truth, it reveals itself over the course of time, despite our best attempts to keep it covered. All of us have things that we like and dislike about ourselves. However, we forget that even if we have traits that we don't like, we have the power to fix them. If issues go unaddressed and we continue the cycle of choosing superficially, your "to be or not to be" will be affected. When you want someone or something for all the wrong reasons, you must accept the fact that this may not be your "to be."

Happiness should not be something we only experience externally. Although it can be enhanced by a person, it should not come only because of them. We can't begin this pursuit of happiness by pretending to be in a place where we have not arrived ourselves. We need internal joy first and then we can start to enjoy it in a relationship. The truth of the matter is, if there is unresolved bitterness, resentment, hurt, and unforgiveness within you, you probably should not be seeking a relationship. The greater desire should be wholeness. We must face the reality that there is needed work that has to be done before we can build another relationship.

Imagine someone is buying land and begins building on top of the existing rubble without doing any research about the foundation. After starting the work, they find issues with what lies underneath, which was not exposed to the physical eye. Any reputable contractor would advise the builder to survey the land underneath to ensure the foundation is secure enough to support what's being built on top. It may take more time, it may cost more money, it may even take more resources, but it's worth it!

Failure to take the necessary precautions will often result in having to restart a project because of what is found during a deep inspection. Although the builder looks forward to the final sign-off of the project, it's important to note that every project has intermediate inspections to ensure that the progress made is according to code and not based only on what you want. Based on the code, the inspector will either sign off on your project or will tell you what changes you need to make. Here is where you have to be honest: are you building relationships without surveying the land? Are you performing intermediate inspections while getting to know someone to ensure the person you are attempting to be with is "up to code?" How have you responded when you discover something that is not up to code? STOP! If one of the

Side note:
The preparation for what's to come is more important than accepting your "to be" ill prepared.

steps to recovery is to admit what is wrong, then the process of understanding my "to be" has to begin with me.

It's not surprising that many people question if they'll ever get married or if marriage is for them. Something I learned from my previous marriage is that the goal should be to be happily married, not just married. That was a complete mindset shift from what I'd seen as I was growing up and even from what I saw as an adult. I have witnessed people who were married and unfaithful for years; people who were married for years but were not friends and people who were married but unhappy. What was surprising was that all of these people were still married!

Before getting married and during my first marriage, I remember desiring what I call "IT." Years after my divorce and living a bachelor life again, I was desiring "IT" even more. I experienced wonderful women who walked in and out my life, all because I was not ready to commit. I damaged them all because my pain was unaddressed and I was still unclear about how "IT" would look.

I enjoyed the single life, but I still longed for "IT." "IT" is the thing that most of us search for and spend what feels like a lifetime trying to figure out how to obtain. You envision how "IT" might look, how "IT" might feel, and sometimes you sense that you finally have "IT." "IT" can be confusing. You may think that "IT" has to be a certain height, a certain size, or of a certain status. Searching for "IT" causes most of us to miss opportunities to be happy. We will never be happy with finding someone who goes against our idea of "IT," if "IT" is all that matters. I vividly remember the agony of knowing I was missing "IT" and how strongly I craved "IT." But I could only equate "IT" to wanting to feel love and to be affirmed. It was much after the divorce that I discovered that the "IT" I looked for in a woman was the thing I failed to find in myself. There were many times when I was asked what went wrong with my first marriage. My excuse rested with the fact I felt my ex-wife did not know how to love me.

While married, I know my ex-wife attempted to love me. I experienced her love, yet I still felt like I was missing "IT." I ended up playing the blame game and pointing the finger at my ex-wife, rather than understanding how major my role was in destroying our marriage. It comes down to cause and effect. Although we

Side note: Sometimes our ability to see the truth can be clouded because we're in our feelings.

are good friends now, that came long after the divorce and after many honest conversations. Like me, how many of us have spent years in and out of relationships, years in marriages, or years of singleness with an indescribable craving to have "IT?" I spent years exerting time and energy only to discover the riddle of finding "IT" remains an unsolved mystery if you're not willing to examine yourself. Although I was reluctant to admit how much I was confused about not understanding "IT" and how not having "IT" made me feel, I better understand now that the search for "IT" starts in me. It has been said that hindsight is 20/20 and I concur. It was not until after the divorce that I began truly working on understanding what "IT" is and how to acquire it.

I spent years wondering if my "IT" was meant to be. I went through the mental battle of thinking that something was wrong with me until I realized that the "IT" I was seeking was simply a reflection of the part of me that includes *Intimacy Beyond the Bedroom.* "IT" is when you know what you know, you are where you are, yet you feel a sense of self-worth. "IT" is the value you bring to the table and gratification of owning your happiness.

Now remarried, I discovered much of what I wanted others to provide me was a false expectation on my part. I now see how immaturity played a negative role in my short and long-term relationships. I can recall the particular counseling session when my ex-wife stated, "I never wanted to marry a preacher." I felt those words would never be erased from my memory. How could my "to be" say this, when she knew about my calling before we were married? Some of the difficulties we experienced in our marriage often took me back to her words. To me, those words carried a negative connotation with them. All I wanted was for her to want to be married to me, as a person, and the part of me who was a pastor.

As difficult as it was to pretend like everything was fine at home, at church and in our marriage, the journey to healing did not begin until my ex-wife and I admitted that our attempts to stay together were not working. This was not an easy thing to admit to others, and it was even harder to admit it to ourselves. When we try to survive in relationships, friendships, or marriages, with scarce communication, no vulnerability and no trust, it is essentially relationship suicide.

My true struggle, I found, was not with people. It was not being in tune with me enough to accept where I was in my journey. My "IT" is mine to own. That internal connection supersedes financial status, social status and any of the other "boxes " everyone so desperately wants to check when meeting someone. Everyone's "IT" is individual and specific to you. What is your "IT?"

CHAPTER

ELEVEN

"What happens when you don't know you well enough to distinguish what you need from what you want?
Knowing others is wisdom, knowing yourself is enlightenment."
Lao Tzu

The (INNER ME)

Sometimes the thoughts and behaviors inside of us are the very things that work against us. Another lesson I've learned is that time does not always equate to evolution. As time passes, you would think that we will make better decisions, but unfortunately, that is not always the case. Time can pass and things can, and will, remain the same if you continue to "fail the test."

Failures and mistakes allowed me to recognize that there was something deeper in me that I'd been hiding from others. This realization was locked away behind my ego, behind my pride, and behind all the insecurities I had. I realize how inadequate I was and how most of my issues were internal, having nothing to do with other people. Not only were there issues with myself, but there were also issues within myself.

Sidenote: As much as I want to contribute what I know to the passing of time, I'll be the first to admit that what I learned was because of failure and many mistakes.

I experienced a major mindset shift when I finally learned that time does not heal all wounds. It was then that I understood that it takes effort, in addition to time, to experience positive change. The INNER ME is where I found that I housed all my insecurities, inadequacies, and uncertainties. This is the place where I housed unaddressed issues of my past. Growing up, I observed so many people with real issues, blame the fact that they had issues on the enemy, or in the church world, the devil. It was after praying, after believing God and after much reflection, I knew it was the INNER ME. There were moments when I found myself fasting and praying, but still battling past wounds, past hurts, and past memories. For years, I held on to my truth of how I wished things were different with my parents and my grandparents. I wondered why this was my path and not someone else's. As result, I would argue and get very upset with women over small, inconsequential things because I was really angry at those who let me down when I was a child. I hadn't learned how to deal with being corrected by a woman, how to be patient, or how to listen with the intent to understand. There were times that my ex-wife had no clue what was going on with the INNER ME.

How often do you find yourself getting mad at someone else for the battle that goes on in your "Inner Me?" Do you ever feel embarrassed for letting a situation get the best of you? How often do you get mad at a friend, a family member, or your spouse without revealing the real reason for your anger? As crazy as it sounds, I spent more time helping others improve themselves and their relationships than I did on evaluating my unhappiness. I ignored the greater need to assist the INNER ME with my problems and focused on others. Being married for almost 10 years taught me that even if a person can add to your happiness, if your INNER ME is not happy, it is not enough to make the relationship work. I realize now that my inability to be honest about my INNER ME was what caused a deficiency in the relationships around me. After the divorce, instead of focusing on bettering myself, I blamed my ex-wife. I placed the blame on her to avoid taking responsibility for the role I played in destroying our marriage. At one point, I was single and seeing multiple women at one time, and still miserable. I was so busy juggling relationships that I had no time to focus on my INNER ME. On the outside, it seemed like I enjoyed my singleness. The truth was that I kept individuals around me to disguise the loneliness. When I evaluated other relationships, it didn't take much work to help them. However, when it came to dealing with myself, it was a completely different story. The work I needed seemed endless!

It was after I had been single for about three years, running good women away and refusing to work on my INNER ME, when I knew something had to change. The ending of 2017 was really life changing. Although I didn't tell anyone, I had a constant battle with thoughts of suicide.

Sidenote: There are some things that will make you contemplate life itself if you allow it to stay inside of you.

I had to fight to get out of bed. I avoided going around people and I pretended like I was fine. Working on my INNER ME became a daily fight. This was fought in public, in private and even in the presence of people at my church who thought that I was okay. Still, I kept going to church and kept pretending to practice my faith, but I was not getting better. I was still dealing with my INNER ME. In another attempt to avoid being home alone, I started hanging out, listening to live music. I love live music and it quickly became a sedative to help me go to sleep when I returned home. I would often arrive early and wait in the car because I had nowhere else to go. I would come in late so that others wouldn't realize how desperate I was to be out of my house. Throughout the week, I found different spots to go to every night. I would go to work the next morning or go to church on Sunday, and it looked like I was having the time of my life. Is it just me or are there moments when you are out and everyone is having fun, yet you question why you are there?

As valuable as you are, make sure you're careful about people who do not understand the difference between covering you and covering up for you. Covering up includes making excuses for you, allowing you to live below your potential, and not pushing you to be the best you can be. As opposed to, people who cover you demonstrate they care about who you are, are supportive of what you do, stand with you in good or bad times, and offer you support that helps you get to where you're going. They are invested in you not because of what they can get

> **Sidenote:**
> There are moments where we end up in places that are meant to reveal the truth about ourselves.

out of you, but because of what they see in you. That cycle — me going out listening to live music and living a bachelor's life —lasted around three and a half years. It was all to avoid dealing with my INNER ME. Night after night, woman after woman, I felt that things were still not getting better for me. I was occupied, but covering up the fact that I was still lonely. At the end of 2018, I acquired a DUI after happy hour one night. I was taken into custody and I spent a night in jail. That night in jail forced me to take a hard look at the INNER ME.

Sidenote: The people around you shouldn't be there to cover up for you, but to cover you when you need it.

The more truthful I was to my INNER ME, the greater the chance I had of truly having peace. However, I realized that the INNER ME is the part of me that can be deceptive, both intentionally and unintentionally. People tell you to trust your heart. But how can you trust in something that is deceptive at times? Trust comes only after you've done the work to declutter the issues that are clogging your major artery.

The INNER ME is made up of both the heart and mind, and it matters more than I cared to admit. I didn't know that many of my choices started off with things buried in my INNER ME, from the past to the present, both good and bad. I remember thinking that *Intimacy Beyond the Bedroom* would be easy. I thought I saw so many bad examples of intimacy that it would be easy to improve on the mistakes of the people I observed. I thought that as long as I put forth the effort, *Intimacy Beyond the Bedroom* would come naturally. I even got to the point where I forgot that every experience, as awful as it might have been, had to deal with the core of my INNER ME. Many of us have seen and felt years of anger and resentment, verbal or non-verbal abuse, a lack of communication, domestic violence, molestation, and more. With every experience, there is some residue that remains inside of us. You have to do the work to cleanse yourself regardless how long it takes.

The desire to understand your INNER ME is a good way to begin discovering *Intimacy Beyond the Bedroom*. How often have you tried to explain to someone that your craving wasn't physical? How often have you spared someone's feelings, by hiding and ignoring your truth, knowing something more was missing? I was ashamed to admit how much of my past truth contributed to the man I had become during that time. The man I am today understands that there is power behind knowing and admitting your truth. For example, my siblings and I were in the same childhood situation resulting in emotional challenges, and those challenges have affected our individual families and relationships in different ways. Although all of my brothers, except one, have been married, we all also went through the trauma of a divorce. We don't try to use our childhoods as an excuse, but the question must be asked: how much of what we went through has affected our ability to have successful relationships?

The truth is that without healing, many people treat people the way we have been treated in the past, whether this is in other relationships, friendships, and even with our children. The more I've come to grips with my INNER ME, the better I treat those who are important to me. There was a time in my early adult life where I felt I could love without limits and other times when I felt inadequate. The feeling of inadequacy not only affected my previous marriage, but it touched multiple areas of my life. When dealing with matters of the heart, you have to know the difference between actions and intentions. You have to know yourself well enough to understand what you can handle.

There were times when I refused to reveal the INNER ME because I didn't trust the intentions of the person. Most of us can't even begin to start dealing with true intimacy within ourselves because we are too afraid of, "what if." What if I open myself up and end up getting hurt? What if I trust the wrong person? What if I invest my energy and it ends up being a waste of time? Fear will have you over thinking your own insecurities, while missing out on amazing possibilities. Owning your truth provides power over what others may think or say.

Before we can allow ourselves to open up to people who have good intentions, we have to be intentional about getting to know our own INNER ME. To do this, you must be honest with yourself, about yourself, before making a commitment to someone else.

Side note:
If you believe a person has a good heart, but their actions continue to show their unwillingness to grow, then you have a choice to make.

I remember while dating my wife, there were many conversations about the future, marriage, and our future dreams and goals. Both of us shared where we believed we were headed in life, what we wanted in a relationship, where we saw ourselves professionally, and even what we experienced in our past. I vividly remember sharing my INNER ME with her and how vulnerable it felt. Likewise, she shared her previous experiences, pain and areas of struggle. What may appear as simple conversations, were moments of intimacy shared between two individuals that extended beyond the bedroom. How many people can say they know you versus knowing things about you? When you truly experience *Intimacy Beyond the Bedroom*, those insecurities and uncertainties which controlled you in the past, start to melt away willingly without feeling forced. Sharing your INNER ME will seem like a roller coaster ride. A simple conversation can take you from a place of crying, to soul-bursting laughter, and end at a place of validation.

> **Side note:**
> If people really knew my INNER ME, they would know that I used to disguise what I was feeling by making others laugh. Now, I make people laugh because I learned that laughter is medicine for the soul.

The point I want to drive home here is that so many of us blame individuals for how things are in our lives. After further review of your INNER ME, you may find that the thing that needs to change resides in you.

CHAPTER TWELVE

"Not everything that is faced can be changed, but nothing can be changed until it is faced."
James Baldwin

BACK TO BASICS

What core truths have you abandoned or ignored in order to get what you wanted? Whether you believe in the bible or not, there are some amazing principles to life we can extract, just as we can from other inspirational books. In the beginning of time, it describes a story about Adam and Eve and how the Creator placed Adam in the Garden and communed with him daily. Adam, being in tune with himself, fully enjoyed the physical and spiritual place where he resided. As he spent time talking to and walking daily in an intimate relationship with his Creator, he experienced peace. Adam found himself focusing on cultivating his surroundings instead of allowing the appearance of something missing to alter his focus. The bible describes how every creature had a mate, except Adam. Can you imagine the type of intimacy that allowed Adam to be so productive, to the point where he experienced fulfillment that came from being productive and seeing the results of his labor? Let me suggest that Adam was not only intimate with his Creator, but he spent time appreciating who he was and what he had.

There's a passage of scripture that describes how Adam was in the garden sharing intimate time with God and how God walked with him in the cool of the day. This was the time when Adam had no wants and never truly noticed anything missing in his life. Everything in him and around him was perfect because he experienced so much inner peace. This peace had nothing to do with sex, money, or another person. He experienced no lack. Before Eve was created, Adam was not concerned with sex, dating, or trying to find the perfect person. Adam was focused on his responsibilities of naming the animals and cultivating the land. He was completely focused on that internal purpose that held more weight than the physical aspects of his life. Adam found himself occupied daily, being mindful of his goals and purpose and that brought him fulfillment. By tilling the garden (work) and taking care of his responsibility (naming the animals), Adam experienced an intimacy that most of us miss because we are not walking in the wholeness given to us by our Creator. Being whole and at peace in our INNER ME is what we all crave. When we fail to address our issues, we settle for external short-lived companionship, rather than pursuing intimacy that comes with being whole.

Sidenote:
If the person who comes into your life does not add to the value you already have, you'll soon find yourself living with less than you deserve.

Adam was so occupied being productive, that he never felt lonely. It was God who brought it to his attention, when He said, "It is not good for man to be alone," and made him a help meet. After creating the woman from Adam's side, they continued living in the same peace Adam had before she arrived.

Adam and Eve experienced intimacy at a level that, although they were naked, exposed, and uncovered, they didn't concern themselves with flaws or their appearance. After being warned about the knowledge from the Tree of Good and Evil, it was their own decision that allowed them to partake of the fruit. Notice here that there's no blame game. Yes, Eve offered Adam the fruit, but Adam had a choice not to take it.

Their actions exposed them to another type of knowledge. The story goes on to talk about how God came to look for them to continue the intimate time He experienced with them every day. However, He found them in a state that He had not desired for them. God asked the question, "Where art thou?" That was the first question God asked man about his state. Something was different, abnormal, and out of place. God noticed the place where He left Adam and Eve was not the place where He found them. They hid, and then covered themselves because of their embarrassment. This is so rich in context because at times we do the same thing. How many times have you tried to cover up how bad that relationship was? How many times have you

Sidenote:
No one can take you where you're unwilling to go; if you say yes, you have to accept responsibility for participating.

made excuses for the other person? How many times have you realized the truth, but was not willing to accept it was a bad decision?

They were in a different place spiritually and emotionally. Although they were still in a physical garden, they opened themselves up to spiritual things that they would not have known if Adam had obeyed the commandment to not eat off that tree. How hard does that hit home? If you would've just listened to your INNER ME, you could've avoided all the hurt and disconnection from your place of peace.

When God found Adam, He asked him, "Who told you that you were naked?" It took me many years to understand the place Adam found himself in was the same place from which I was trying to bounce back from. A place where you don't like what has happened, but also don't know what to do about it. Like a lot of us, I desired something or someone more valuable than what I had. It is unfortunate that we allow other people and things in our lives to lead us away from our true place of peace only to experience disappointment, and brokenness. We will always be left asking, "Why me?"

Like Adam, so often we try to operate like we're whole, when we're still broken. We take our brokenness and we try to build with broken people only to find ourselves in unstable relationships. I remember someone told me that two halves make a whole. However, life has since taught me that two whole people make a wholesome relationship.

The story of Adam shows us what happens when we lose our focus or purpose, because we're in our feelings. It was not just his status that changed, but he allowed his desire to please Eve to override the peace he experienced before her. Like Adam, I see how craving a physical connection too much will jeopardize your peace. Both Adam and Eve learned how one action, one connection, one decision can change your destiny. One decision caused them to experience something they had never experienced before. They experienced what disconnection felt like and now they were in desperate need to get that intimacy back.

Whether intentional or unintentional, we all have made decisions in the past that we wished we made differently. We try to bury those decisions deep in our hearts and minds. Regardless of the attempt, they cannot be hidden from our true identity.

The truth is that pursuing *Intimacy Beyond the Bedroom* with oneself initially does not always feel good. It causes you to stop settling for anything and refuse to move into another relationship, until you take the necessary time to process and understand what you truly desire. It was only after years of pretending to be happy and not being honest that I finally understood from where fulfillment comes. The fulfillment missing in my life was not predicated on a person, but rather, it depended on me being honest and happy with myself.

For me it was after the divorce, after dating multiple women, and after being sexual with them, that I realized the only person I needed to get to know more about was myself. When we're alone, we have to deal with being lonely without people distracting us from the need to deal with our issues. Many people use the term *lonely* to define where they are or what they feel. Let me point out that there is a major difference between a person who doesn't want to be alone and the person who can't be alone. It's the point where we realize that true fulfillment does not come from simply having someone, but it comes from you being happy with yourself first.

Before my first marriage, I thought my fulfillment would come when I finally decided to get married, purchase a home, and have kids. Unfortunately, that was not the case and far from the truth. After I got married, bought my first home, and had kids, I was left thinking that there had to be more to life. Although external things assist in fulfillment, there's a greater appreciation when fulfillment is experienced as a result of the internal work you've put into your INNER YOU.

I learned, the hard way, that the person I needed to make me happy was the person I saw in the mirror every day. Realizing this led me on an internal mission to a deeper place of knowing myself. Again, not only time, but with effort, I finally reached the place where my longing for companionship did not override my ability to find fulfillment in myself.

Intimacy Beyond the Bedroom is not about pretending to be fulfilled. It comes down to understanding who we are and what our purpose is before choosing a companion with whom you would like to share your happiness. We must understand who we are and what we need before we enter into relationships. We need to realize that a person cannot do for us what we have yet to do for ourselves. *Intimacy Beyond the Bedroom* is not found because of a relationship with someone. It comes from being happy with you, your experiences and being secure in yourself.

Back to basics simply means that at the core of

who you are, and what you expect, should not be determined by someone outside of you. It is wonderful to desire marriage and a family. It is noble to want to own a house and be successful in your career. Just remember, there are people who have all those things and more, yet they remain unfulfilled. The pursuit for fulfillment should end up with you being in a place where you experience irreplaceable peace. The kind of peace, that makes us as individuals so much greater than our desire to allow external things to make us lose sight of our truth. Had Adam walked in his truth, his experience would have led him down a completely different path. Unlike Adam, many of us have to determine that the place we're in, is so much greater than allowing a person to deter us from the peace we have come to know.

When things don't go according to our plans, people tend to believe that just because one chapter finishes it means that the story is over. I can attest that no matter how something starts, there's still time to write the next chapter of your life. No matter how bad it appears at the time, you can still experience fulfillment. The type of fulfillment where desire does not control you, but you control your desire.

As much as we don't like to start over, some people do better alone than attaching to someone you have to lower your standards to accommodate. Insecure individuals have a way of highlighting your flaws to make themselves feel better about their own inadequacies. There are times when we allow feelings to get in the way of decisions we need to make to get "US" to a better place. Other times, things are finished long before they end, which we are only able to admit after much pain. I have been remarried for almost two years now. I look back over the past two years and see many eye-opening lessons.

Many issues will never be resolved until we have the courage to face the hard reality of a situation. Although my wife and I were equally excited about our future, there were people around us who felt like we were rushing into a union and not taking all things into consideration, like our children from previous relationships and the impact our decision to marry will have on other areas of our lives. As much as we believed and expressed our awareness of all things considered, we later found out that just because one chapter of our lives finished didn't mean that it would no longer impact us.

Side note: Any issues you avoid addressing will come back full circle.

Past issues can lie dormant until they manifest themselves in our conversation, actions, and thoughts in our new circumstances.

During the first year of my current marriage, we uncovered so much about each other that we that both assumed there was nothing left to discover. However, we were able to encourage each other to receive individual counseling so we could better understand the impact past issues have on our marriage. We both admit that our past has had its impact on the way we operate. We found out that my wife is a very affectionate person and is now married to a person who does not always display, nor need a whole lot of affection. This has tested our relationship and requires compromise. Now, I am more affectionate than I have ever been. However, the amount of time you are married to a person does not equate to the strength of your relationship; what you put in, will determine what you get out of it.

In the past, I talked about being done with dating because it took so much work to get to know someone, only for it to not work out. Now that I am married again, I realize that I still have to do work to get to know my wife and to allow her to know the real me. I find that many of us are quick to say what we want and don't want, but what we fail to understand is the reason why. What are the reasons behind why you respond the way you do, why your mood goes up and down, why you are as affectionate as you are,

> **Sidenote**: Although you think you know someone, it's not until you've spent time with them that you find out what is really on the inside .

why you're a loner, why you're not as expressive, why you're able to move on or keep people around longer than needed and more? The reasons why you're not where you want to be might not fall on someone else. The truth is yours to own. How many times has the relationship ended, but the disappointment was not over? Yes, the marriage is finished, but how deep it hurts is not over. Yes, the experience is over, but the impact it has on your life is not over. Yes, you're an adult, but the pain you endured during your childhood is not over.

One of the primary goals of *Intimacy Beyond the Bedroom* is to help individuals come to grips with past decisions, present conditions, and future expectations.

Each of these must be settled inwardly before you can experience what comes with knowing true *Intimacy Beyond the Bedroom*. I understand now more than I ever have that how things start is not the way they have to finish. After my divorce, I was so over relationships and marriage. But now, in my current marriage I realize I still have to work on the same issues I failed to address in my previous marriage, only now with a different mindset.

I was finished with commitments, compromise and pursuing companionship. I was finished with having to sacrifice and support. I was finished with trying and I was done feeling lonely. In my mind, there was nothing further to be said about marriage and no one could convince me otherwise. Yet, after all the self-help books, many counseling sessions — both Christian and secular — I realized that things came down to my thinking and how I processed information. Yes, knowing is half the battle, but the ability to take what you know to help you deal with your issues goes a long way.

Two people can go through the same situation and come out with completely different views and it all depends on their thinking. Many people who are in new situations sometimes revert back to who they were before, if there is no change in their mindset. This is especially true when situations are similar to what we've gone through in the past. As much as you try to approach these situations with a different perspective, we often can't help but to go back to what we know when we are out of our comfort zone. We tend to draw back to feel safe and to protect ourselves from disappointment and letdown. I was known to quickly revert when I was faced with a situation that I experienced in the past. People who revert want more, but they are not willing to expose their heart and share their life. They are afraid of being hurt and make every effort to avoid the same negative outcome from their past. One characteristic of people who revert is that they won't open up without enough assurance from the person they decide to invest their time and energy into. It's not hard to find ourselves reverting back to a place of safety in relationships when things appear to be wrong. Have you noticed how much harder it is to change when you naturally revert? The struggle is not with the person; it's an internal battle. Mindset matters when it comes to addressing the patterns of a person who reverts. They are often so cautious that they are too worried about getting hurt to try something new.

Back to basics is not just about getting back to a good place and getting back to the feeling you had before going through a painful experience; it's about understanding the core of who you are and appreciating the value in knowing you. Additionally, it's about putting forth the effort to recognize the work you need to do is not something behind you, around you, or can be done without you; it's in you. *Intimacy Beyond the Bedroom* is attained when you're able to admit what you have gone through, and are

> **Sidenote**:
> Nothing can be achieved unless we're willing to be vulnerable.

willing to take the time to leave your baggage in the past, refusing to carry negative feelings and thoughts into your future. This can all be done; it's mind over matter! While you may be alone, that doesn't have to end with you being lonely. When you look at your life, remember that where you are and what you've become, could be a result of your choices. Always remember that just because a chapter finishes, it does not mean that the story is over.

Through all the lessons I have learned, one sticks out more than most. After blaming so many people for not being what I needed, and after many temporary and short-lived companionships, the biggest issue was not with anyone else. The problem all along was ME.

If you're in a relationship, if you're single, or on a quest to find your happily ever after, before you take another step, before you waste another day, take note that you are worth getting to know. Once you know you better, then and only then will you experience *Intimacy Beyond the Bedroom*.

Sidenote:
You have to allow yourself time to learn, make mistakes, and grow.

KEY STEPS TO DISCOVERING
INTIMACY BEYOND THE BEDROOM?

1.Realize the doors that you have yet to unlock.
2.Use your keys and discover what's behind the real you.
3.Clean the room (address your issues).
4.Realize what you need to keep and what you need to discard of.
5.Realize the value of having and owning those keys.
6.Remember getting to know you is invaluable!

ABOUT THE AUTHOR

"I learned so much about myself the more time I spent alone. The pain of being left without forced me to focus inwardly on several things I misunderstood about myself."
Elton Penn

Elton Penn is a charismatic teacher, preacher, and author who is passionate about strengthening relationships and helping people pursue wholeness. With over 22 years of experience as a life coach, this Southern California native started from a place of brokenness. After experiencing divorce, now remarried, Elton has managed to ascertain the formula: Renewed Mindset + Consistent Effort = Wholeness.

Elton holds a Bachelor's degree in Christian Counseling and a Master's degree in Religious Education. He is also the CEO of World Centered Outreach, a non-profit organization that assists youth transitioning out of the foster care system. Elton is a community leader known for his impact on families. One of the principles by which he governs himself is, "Laughter is medicine for the soul."

Elton lives in Long Beach, California, with his beautiful wife and life partner, Quiana. As a result of their blended family, he is the father to eight amazing children. Life experiences, mistakes, pain and victories have all fueled his passion for seeing individuals, as well as couples, realize the power of acknowledging and addressing their issues, as opposed to ignoring them. It is his sincerest desire that his first published book, *Intimacy Beyond the Bedroom*, would focus less on pointing fingers and more on learning to own your truth.

For more information, speaking engagements, bulk book orders, or to contact Elton, please visit:

www.AuthorEltonPenn.com

Connect with Elton on social media:

@AuthorEltonPenn

www.ingramcontent.com/pod-product-compliance
Lightning Source LLC
Chambersburg PA
CBHW071446090426
42737CB00011B/1800